Praise for Cindy Solomon

"Cindy Solomon has been a gift to our organization and our customers. She has reenergized our organization's focus on exceptional guest service and leadership. Her real world knowledge, humor and passion were just what we needed."

— HEATHER YOUNG
EXECUTIVE DIRECTOR OF HUMAN RESOURCES,
TELLURIDE SKI & GOLF

"Cindy is wise, funny, entertaining, inspiring and profoundly understanding of issues that face professionals who are trying to keep many balls in the air."

— ANN MESSENGER
PRESIDENT, MESSENGER ASSOCIATES, INC.

"Cindy's program on customer service leadership is exceptional. The content Cindy shared was surpassed only by her style and talent as a speaker. She is smart, dynamic, entertaining, and engaging. I look forward to my next opportunity to participate in one of her programs."

— MARIE D. DiSANTE
MANAGING PARTNER, CARLTON DiSANTE & FREUDENBERGER LLP

"Cindy, you are the "bomb"!! Everybody loved your presentation! Your refreshing topic on the challenges we face and mustering the courage to make change was right on target both professionally and personally for the audience. Your humorous delivery energized and motivated everyone."

— STEVEN JACKSON
DIRECTOR, CAREER DEVELOPMENT/ROP,
SONOMA COUNTY OFFICE OF EDUCATION

"Cindy spoke for the second year in a row at our WISE Conference. She is the dynamite that hits the stage each year and sets the place on fire! Our audience of close to 1,000 women waits on her every word, every year. Cindy "gets" the reason any good business person is in business—for the love of the customer!"

— JOANNE LENWEAVER
DIRECTOR, WISE CENTER, WHITMAN SCHOOL OF MANAGEMENT

"This was the most motivational presentation I have ever seen in 20 years at my company. Cindy helped motivate me to do things differently for myself, my company and my customers."

— ATTENDEE, ELI LILLY NATIONAL MEDICAL
INFORMATION CONFERENCE

The RULES of WOO

An Entrepreneur's Guide to
Capturing the Hearts & Minds of
Today's Customers™

Cindy Solomon

publishers

One Plane Ride Publishers
San Francisco

FIRST EDITION

Published by OPR Publishers
112 Elsie Street, San Francisco, CA 94110

Interior Design by 1106 Design
Cover Design by VW-Graphics.com

Publisher's Cataloging-in Publication Data

Solomon, Cindy.
    The Rules of Woo: An Entrepreneur's Guide to Capturing the Hearts & Minds of Today's Customers™ /Cindy Solomon;—1st ed.
        p. cm.
    Includes bibliographical references
    ISBN 978-0-9826728-0-8 (alk. paper)
        1. Customer Service. 2. Small Business. 3. Customer Loyalty

Library of Congress Control Number: 2010925298

*For Beth and Emma who help me
reach for success every day.*

Contents

Author's Note

I grew up hearing about entrepreneurs. My father worked for the one he thought was the most impressive of all. Mr. Paul Seifert. Mr. Seifert (as we were taught to call him) owned one of the largest automobile dealerships in the West. He was not only wildly successful in the 1950s automotive market but also incredibly well known in his community for his generous contributions and fundraising. Mr. Seifert was, in my father's eyes, the best example of a business-person that you could find. Not only was he successful but he also looked out for others, including my father.

Family lore has it that my father started working for Mr. Seifert as a shag boy—cleaning cars and moving them around on the lot. Through pure hard work and street smarts he eventually worked his way up to become president of Seifert Pontiac. Family lore being what it is, I would guess that most of this story is true but parts have been embellished over the years. The most impor-tant embellishment, in my mind, is that it *only* takes hard work to become a great entrepreneur. If that were really true, a lot more people would make it to the top.

Of course nothing in life is that simple. Today, creating a successful business requires much more than elbow grease. Certainly it takes a belief in your product or service. A belief in the people with whom you surround yourself. And a belief in your ability to defy the odds. But it also requires you to be skilled at choosing the right priorities and, perhaps most importantly, it requires you to have the courage to become involved in the lives of the people you depend on most for your livelihood, your customers and your employees.

That's what this book is all about. I used to joke that I wanted to become the speaker and consultant I wish I could have hired when I started out. This is the book I wish I could have read when I first started my company. It's a guide that, I hope, will help you build rewarding partnerships with the customers who suit your business best and enable you to achieve the success you so richly deserve.

Introduction: Why We Must Woo

For over 35 years I have worked around the country and across industries. I have worked inside Fortune 100 companies as a top executive. And I have run my own business for nearly two decades. I have guided teams of thousands and teams of one. I have worked with exceptional leaders who create amazing cultures and others who destroy them. I have witnessed the emergence of passionate entrepreneurs who go on to great heights and have observed the agony of the end of entrepreneurial dreams.

I have watched as technology has given birth to a new world order ... in our lives, in our businesses and in our communities. I have ridden the information wave and fought to digest its data at ever increasing rates. I have managed businesses through economic downturns, terrorist attacks and more client changes than I care to remember. I have celebrated extraordinary wins with my team and sacrificed countless hours of sleep over the losses.

Yet through it all one thing has always remained true. No matter what you sell, who you sell it to, what industry you are in, what size your company is, or how long you have been in business—your success relies on one insistent, demanding, delightful, pernicious, exciting, terrifying, unfathomable and uncontrollable constant: your customers. It is on your customers' shoulders that your success as an entrepreneur rests. And yet, as I look across the hundreds of organizations with whom I have worked as well as the thousands of businesses I have dealt with as a customer, I am constantly stunned by the sheer number of those who *talk* about customers being important and yet their everyday actions show those same customers ... how *un*important they really are.

Think of your latest bad customer service experience and you'll know exactly what I mean. Think of the last time you walked into your local drug store or tried to get a question answered by your insurance company. Did you feel valued? Taken care of? Even noticed? Because of what I do for a living, I ponder these questions daily and treat nearly every interaction I have with human beings and their technological surrogates as an opportunity to learn. I can tell you the news isn't good. Even during our latest economic meltdown, when you might imagine most companies would be paying particular attention to the details of serving and keeping their customers, it seems things just got worse. There are, of course, bright spots. A few companies are hitting the customer service ball out of the park daily. They are proving that service is not a *cost* of doing business but rather it is the engine that drives profitability, efficiencies and long-term business sustainability.

"It is not the strongest of the species that survives, nor the most intelligent. But the one most responsive to change."
— *Charles Darwin*

Darwin's sentiment could not be truer for businesses today. As customers have become more demanding, more educated and are offered more choices than ever before, it has become incumbent upon us as business owners to not only find new and innovative ways to serve them but also to change the way we court them. To survive, we can no longer afford to simply sell to, serve or satisfy our customers. To emerge victorious from this latest evolution in our marketplace, we must become experts at *wooing* them. The good news is these same ruthlessly opinionated customers are quite willing to be wooed. In fact, they're demanding it. Today's customers are eager to put in the effort required to build lasting, mutually rewarding relationships with you—as long as you're willing to do your part too. These relationships, once forged, can be indefinitely rewarding for both parties. As we'll see in some of the examples in this book, investing your time and energy in properly wooing your customers can indeed bring you the success you seek—or at the very least it can make you fall in love with what you do all over again.

Imagine having relationships with your customers that are so secure that they are as invested in your success as you are. Imagine maintaining an ongoing dialogue with your customers about what you are doing well and what you aren't doing well—a conversation that provides you with the very information you need to create more profitability from your relationships with them. Sounds like heaven doesn't it? Believe it or not, as an entrepreneur, you are more likely than most to be able to create this kind of relationship because your passion for your business is also a personal passion for you.

I first began thinking about the concept of wooing customers when I was still working on the other side of the table in corporate America. During this time I collected extensive experience working with customers in senior roles in sales and marketing. Even more enlightening was my work with one of the first database building companies in the country. It was during my time working with large corporations and helping them see the value of "getting to know" their customers that I began to see the vital importance of using that information to woo customers to a company ... not just for a one-time transaction, but forever.

The need for us to woo was crystallized for me when I read the industry-shaping book *The Loyalty Effect* by Frederick Reichheld in which he cited a statistic that holds true even today. It finally provided me with the statistical evidence of what I had believed and taught throughout my corporate career. Reichheld interviewed thousands of customers who left or defected from a product or service to go to a similar product or service. He found that 80 percent of these customers who left were actually "satisfied" with their experience.[1] That's right, up to 80 percent of the customers who leave you and go to your competition are actually "satisfied." That means that in order to woo customers to stay with you forever you have to create more than mere satisfaction. You have to find a way to build a relationship that goes far beyond the transaction. To develop a trusting, proactive, profitable and mutually beneficial partnership, you have to make it *personal*.

This book isn't a typical business book. As a matter of fact it probably breaks all the business book rules. My intention is to provide you with examples, ideas and strategies to help you focus your business on providing the right customers with the right experiences to create the right growth for your company. To offer different perspectives and points of view that will allow you to focus on the priorities that will build your profitability and success. I've used examples from all sizes of companies and from a range of industries. I've tried to provide you with the customer's perspective as much as possible to help you apply these same principles to your business. Whenever you come across a "Put Your Customer Hat On" box, I encourage you to take the time to think about the questions posed there. Doing so will help you shorten the distance between your current practices and practices that work to woo your customers.

Some of the rules I mention here pertain to your business more than others but all are worth reading. This book isn't a checklist. Rather it is a series of questions that will help you uncover effective ways of wooing customers for your particular business. I hope you will find these questions worthy of pondering, sometimes challenging and often inspiring. Remember, to woo is a process. It's a pledge, a focus, a promise, a way of doing business and a way of living your life. It is not only something you *should* do for your company and the people who depend on you for their livelihood, it is also a change you *must* be willing to make to ensure your success and survival.

RULE 1

Know Your Own Strength

"Success is achieved by development of our strengths,
not by elimination of our weaknesses."

— Marilyn Vos Savant

"Let the world know you as you are, not as you think
you should be, because sooner or later, if you are posing,
you will forget the pose, and then where are you?"

— Fanny Brice

I was one of those kids who grew quickly. Between the
summer of my 11th and 12th years, in the span of only
six months, I grew from a tall but not abnormal height
of 5'2" to almost 6'0". Needless to say, my brain was challenged to keep up with all that extra body. Not a day, or
sometimes an hour, went by without my falling over my
own feet or bumping into furniture or walls that, just
months earlier, had seemed so far away.

1

It was around this time I remember playing a typical game with my neighborhood pals. (Yes, this is back in the day when we ran around "unsupervised" all day long in the summer.) After a particularly challenging game of something akin to *running around in circles* I affectionately punched my friend Tim in the shoulder. I thought Tim was joking when he almost went down on one knee grabbing his shoulder as though I had hit him with a baseball bat.

No one was laughing, however, when our home phone (an avocado colored touch tone with a cord long enough to wrap around the entire house) rang and my mother's face registered a look of consternation that was directed right at me. I frantically racked my brain trying to remember what I had done during our day of play that could have gotten me into trouble. After the call my mother sat me down and informed me that, as a result of my "playful punch," my pal Tim had ended up with a bruise on his shoulder the size of a tomato and a mother who was looking for an apology. "You don't know your own strength," my mother said to me in a kind but stern tone as she tried to explain that one of the outcomes of my growth spurt was apparently a physical power that I needed to learn how to control. If I wanted to be successful in navigating the currents of my neighborhood gang, I was going to need to learn to use my newfound strength to garner favor and not fear. Once I understood the implications of my growth spurt, I began to learn how to employ my newfound strength to assist those around me. I reached things on high shelves. I hung banners for the school dance. I carried heavy objects. And I provided a protective presence beside smaller friends who felt threatened by other kids.

So what does my growth spurt have to do with entrepreneurship you might ask? It taught me a valuable lesson that benefits me in my career and life to this day. I learned that understanding your true strengths and knowing how to wield them to produce the outcomes you want are essential to your success in business ... and in life. It is this same ability to understand and employ my strengths that has enabled me to successfully run a business through two economic downturns, a cross-country move and numerous client changes. As an entrepreneur, understanding *your* true strengths and the power they give you to woo your customer is the first step toward creating a resilient business that can not only grow steadily but also withstand the inevitable bumps and bruises every business sustains on the path to success.

Identify Your Abilities, Knowledge And Skills

So many business leaders tell me they have a passion for their products or an innate desire to provide service. While these are indeed attributes of any good entrepreneur they're not the *strengths* that make you uniquely qualified to win the hearts and minds of your customers. No company can successfully woo customers into long-term relationships with aspiration, passion and charisma alone. Only finding, nurturing and using your true strengths can create the loyalty you're after. So you've got a great idea, a great product, a new way of providing a service. Maybe you're already successfully providing your products or services but are looking for a way to grow your business. Either way, you've made a decision to embark on an entrepreneurial journey. The first step in that journey is to uncover your strengths—those true differentiators that will set your business up for success and profitable growth.

Your true strengths are a combination of what you bring to the table naturally, what you have gained over the years through your experiences, and your ever-expanding knowledge base about your product and services. These three things combine to create the true strengths of your company. If pursued consciously, they also become your strategic and competitive differentiators.

I became an entrepreneur almost 20 years ago, after a very successful career in corporate America. When I set out on my own, I was crystal clear about my strengths and confident they would be of benefit to my potential clients. First, I had a natural ability (and love) of public speaking. I particularly enjoyed challenging the status quo from a large platform—the larger the audience and the more provocative the message, the better. This ability enabled me to challenge my audience to see their businesses, and the world, from a refreshing, new perspective. But I wasn't operating on public speaking chutzpah alone.

Thanks to a career stint in the country's first consumer database business, I had knowledge and insight into the attitudes and behaviors of consumers. I had seen firsthand how successful companies leveraged this information to inspire true loyalty among their customers, allowing them to build their revenues and their profitability. And finally, I had the leadership expertise and a proficiency in business operations and finance that I acquired during my years running large organizations within corporate America. These skills helped me see the view from "the other side of the table" and enabled me to offer realistic solutions and real world experience to my clients' business challenges.

The combination of these three attributes defined my company's true strengths and therefore my competitive differentiators. Today, when I focus my resources on refining and cultivating my strengths, my business and my relationships with my customers grow right along with those strengths. Whenever I feel like I'm struggling—when my work seems to be harder than it should be or I'm not creating the outcomes I know I can for my customers—I invariably find that I have wandered from my strengths. Working harder doesn't grow your business unless you are working harder at growing your areas of strength.

So what are the natural abilities you bring to *your* company? Are you a great salesperson, a great connector? Maybe you are awesome at the financials, problem solving, or finding technological solutions? What about your knowledge base? Your experiences? What differentiates you from others who do what you do? Once you can answer these questions quickly and with confidence you'll begin to see a clearer path to successfully wooing loyal customers.

Stick With What You Do Best

Often it is your customers themselves who give you the first push down the slippery slope that leads you away from what you do best. "I know this isn't exactly what you guys do," they say, "but we like and trust you so much, we'd love to have you bid on it anyway." Or better yet, a customer comes into your retail establishment asking for a product or service you don't offer but "certainly could ... I mean ... how hard can it really be?"

Avoiding this temptation may seem counterintuitive at first. Many entrepreneurs have launched successful businesses that began with the phrase, "How hard can it really be?" But they weren't necessarily successful because of their blind courage. Chances are, they were successful because the business idea played into their true strengths. Just as many others have had a go at something with the same spirit of adventure ... and failed miserably. What's important to remember is that the moment you try to become something that doesn't leverage your true strengths—the moment you try to become *everything* instead of *something* to your customer—is the moment you lose the focus you will need to grow a resilient business. In your desire to land the contract/get the customer/help a friend, you slowly but surely veer away from your company's strengths.

It's not always customers who lead you astray. When things are going swimmingly for your business it's easy to start dreaming of possibilities ... big wondrous possibilities that lure you away from the very strengths that built the loyal customer base that's feeding your current success. How many times have you let yourself drift from your strengths only to be brought up short when you realized that doing so was costing you time, energy and valuable customers? In fact, there are numerous factors that can cause you to lose sight of your strengths and step off the path to success—a voracious new competitor, a shift in the economy, a cash flow crisis, and especially overconfidence that is fed by a high level of success. Small businesses and entrepreneurs aren't the only ones that can get caught in this trap. You could fill a book with examples of major multi-national corporations that have lost their competitive edge because they wandered from their original strengths.

When Your Focus Wanders—Toyota

Toyota's difficulty in 2010 with extensive recalls for defective accelerators and braking systems is a great example of a leadership team that lost touch with the strengths and characteristics that differentiated their company from the competition. In 2008, *Toyota's* uncompromising dedication to reliability, durability and quality propelled the company to a position as the world's largest automaker, ending a 77-year reign by *General Motors*. The ensuing enthusiasm and over-confidence that resulted from this designation drew *Toyota's* leaders away from the strengths that had earned them this honored position in the first place. Instead of maintaining their focus on consistency of design they brought in new suppliers to meet the increase in market demand and allowed those new suppliers to diverge from the company's strict design consistency standards. They stopped leveraging their strengths for the benefit of their customers and shifted their efforts to maintaining their position as number one in the world.[2]

Without a keen focus on the company's original strengths *Toyota* began thinking like their competitors—the American car industry—and fell right into the substandard quality trap that was the Americans' undoing.[3] If *Toyota's* leaders had simply maintained their focus, they might have avoided the damage to their reputation and created an even stronger position in the marketplace that could have increased consumer desire for their brand tenfold.

Keep Cultivating Your Strengths

Losing sight of your strengths isn't the only possible pitfall here. Failing to *grow* your strengths can cause trouble for your company, too. *Blockbuster*® is a great example of a company that didn't grow its strengths to keep pace with the marketplace. Their key differentiators were accessibility and uniformity. Sure, movie rental stores existed before *Blockbuster.* But they were all different. They carried different titles. They charged different fees. They had limited selections. And often times the video was damaged or unwatchable. *Blockbuster* brought it all together brilliantly under the universally recognizable big blue banner. They made renting a home movie a uniform process that we all could count on. And we were willing to put up with membership fees, commutes to the local store, and late fees just to be in on the action.

Even the folks at *Blockbuster* got comfortable. In 1999, despite the dramatic changes that were occurring in the marketplace, *Blockbuster* was so busy counting their money they stopped looking for ways to leverage their strengths. By this time, the Internet was changing the way we shopped and it certainly was changing our expectations with regard to time and convenience. A little startup called *Amazon*® was showing us that we could buy things from the convenience of our own homes and expect quick, easy delivery right to our doors. The convergence of these new customer expectations and a near universal unrest among customers regarding the perceived outrageous late fees charged by the now dominant *Blockbuster* created a hole in the marketplace that a man named Reed Hastings was all too happy to fill with a home movie rental concept he called *Netflix*®. Suddenly we didn't have to drive to a store. The DVDs came to us. We didn't have to pay late fees or watch movies on a schedule. We could keep a movie as long as we wanted. The selection was huge. And switching was easy.

> "Search companies, which I won't mention by name, tried to do so many things at the same time, they forgot all about search. They either missed the next revolution of search or they created an opening for a Google to enter."
>
> — *Eric Schmidt*

Blockbuster didn't take action until four years—and millions of dollars in losses—later. Today, *Netflix* has solidified its position with 1.9 million DVDs delivered each day to over 10 million subscribers. They continue to maintain their awesome distribution process and grow their strengths. Despite the fact that they have the perfect opportunity to rest on their laurels (even *Wal-Mart®* tried and failed to usurp them) they continue to broaden their distribution strength by offering instantly downloadable DVDs. They know their customers' expectations will be fulfilled as long as they continue to innovate against their strength.

Act From Your Strength—Andavo Travel

Knowing your strengths and keeping a laser focus on cultivating them ensures your survival when there are shifts in the market, when competitors come after your customers, and particularly when your entire industry is flipped upside down. Brenda Rivers, President & CEO of *Andavo Travel (www.andavotravel.com)*, knows this only too well. From the moment Brenda took the reins of *Andavo Travel* in 1989, she saw that the company's business model was tethered to an industry that was on shifting sand. For years, travel agencies had made their money primarily from the commissions awarded by the airlines themselves. In 1989, over 90 percent of all travel agency revenue was derived from the commissions paid by airlines. With a background in real estate and the law, Brenda saw that this model was counterintuitive at best and, at worst, patently unfair to customers. Naturally, travelers wanted the best prices. But the airlines' commissions were based on dollars sold. This meant that, rather than working together in a mutually beneficial manner, the agents and their customers were at odds.

Brenda had been very successful in two other business ventures before taking over at *Andavo Travel*. She felt the secret to her earlier successes had been her philosophy of "people over profits." This way of thinking had allowed her to focus on doing what was right for her customers and her employees first, which created a strong base of deeply loyal customers that enabled her businesses to flourish. Committing what was considered travel industry blasphemy at the time, Brenda began a campaign of transparency with *Andavo Travel's* customers. She pulled the veil off the numbers and showed her corporate clients what the travel agency was making in airline commissions and rebated much of those commission dollars back to her clients. In place of the commissions she implemented a simple per-ticket fee, which remained the same regardless of the dollar cost of the ticket. This ensured that her agents were working to get the best deal for the customers. It also created a more sustainable business model that could withstand industry change. And the industry did indeed change.

With the advent of the Internet and an increase in direct purchases from consumers, the airlines had completely eliminated the commission structure for agencies by 1997. By then however, *Andavo Travel's* transparent and consultative business model was well established. Brenda's agents had already built strong, mutually beneficial client relationships that were anchored by a shared desire to get the most out of the clients' travel budgets. The agency was able to weather the tsunami of change that hit the travel industry. Relying on her people-centered strength, Brenda took

Andavo Travel from $15 million in 1989 to $100 million in 2007. In 2010, she successfully merged with another regional travel company, boosting annual revenues to over $200 million. This was all accomplished during a time when nearly 80 percent of the independent travel agencies in the country closed their doors or went bankrupt. *Andavo Travel's* "We Travel With You" philosophy allowed them not only to survive industry upheaval but also to thrive.

What's the lesson learned? As an entrepreneur, your greatest opportunities come from being crystal clear as to what your strengths are and knowing how to continue to grow those strengths. Keeping your eye on leveraging your strengths for the benefit of your customers, rather than on your competition or on your pocketbook, is the key. If you miss a growth opportunity that's tied to one of your strengths, you leave an opening that your competitors will find hard to resist.

Strength Is A Balancing Act—Jessie et Laurent

Here's a great example of someone whose success was the direct result of understanding and growing her true strengths. Jessie Boucher started her personal chef business more than 30 years ago because she wanted to "bring people back to their dinner tables." Jessie loved cooking and she wanted to make a contribution to society, to make a difference to the world. "You know how you are when you are young," she says. "Idealistically, I thought we could heal the family outward by bringing people back to their dinner table ...

by freeing them from the struggle and the time it takes to prepare healthy, good food and allow them to enjoy each other with time together at the table." Jessie knew her strength was preparing food in an authentic and loving way. "Everything in our organization is aligned to that purpose—from the growers we buy the organic ingredients from to the people who deliver the food to our clients. It's all focused on providing that purity of purpose. And I know our clients feel that."

Jessie began cooking literally as a way to get out of dental school. At first she cooked for people in their homes. Before long she progressed from one client a week to three clients a day. To expand her skills as a chef, Jessie attended a small French cooking school but quickly realized that wasn't enough. She was going to have to go to the source. After a harrowing stint as the only female chef in the competitive kitchen of a restaurant in France, she decided to sample the fare from "the other side of the kitchen door" by eating her way through the French countryside with as many French families as would have her.

The combination of these experiences allowed Jessie to learn both the techniques used by professional French chefs and the love and wholesomeness of food prepared for individual families in the French countryside. During her gustatory journey she also met a fellow chef who would become her business- and life-partner. Since that trip to France in 1985, Jessie's business, *Jessie et Laurent (www.jessieetlaurent.com)* has grown exponentially. As her husband, Laurent, took over more and more of the day-to-day cooking operation Jessie began to realize that, to grow the business toward its original goals, they would need to constantly refine all areas of their operation from food preparation, to packaging, to delivery. Delivering meals to hundreds of families in the San Francisco Bay area every week takes more than skilled cooking; it takes strengths in process, quality assurance, leading a team, etc.

Today Jessie admits that maintaining a balance between growth and working from their strengths is a continual challenge. "At the beginning, I had to grow the business to a certain level so it was profitable enough to keep doing this thing that both Laurent and I loved. Then I found I had to keep getting out of the way so the dream could continue, but on a bigger scale. I had to get out of the kitchen (which I loved) so that Laurent could maximize his strengths and I could focus on my management strengths to keep us on the right path." There are times when Jessie sees additional growth opportunities but she limits the number of customers they can take so that their quality stays true to their vision. "We have times where we have waiting lists of customers. We know we can't keep up our high levels of taste—of innovation, of delivery, of any of our processes—if we grow too quickly or beyond what we know we can deliver with 100 percent quality."

Because *Jessie et Laurent* has been so successful, the business has had myriad competitors enter the marketplace to try to replicate their success. "We've had so many competitors enter the market and go directly after our customers. Most of them are much better funded than we are. But whenever we are hit with significant competition, we don't walk away from our strengths. We look at [the competitors] only to see if we can learn anything that will help us grow those strengths. Every competitor has gone out of business within a year of entering our space."

Start With Your Strength—Roberta Winchell, Attorney

Roberta Winchell started her Bangor, Maine law firm *(www.WinchellLaw.com)* at the beginning of the economic slowdown, which could have been fatal for a new business that specialized in estate planning among other things. Because Roberta launched her business on the foundation of her true strengths, she found success. "I wanted to stay true to my own values," she says. To achieve this goal, Roberta eschewed the typical industry tactics that required ruthless billing, putting the firm's interests above the clients' and treating people differently based on their value to the business. "When I opened my doors I decided to tell the truth even if the advice I gave meant I wouldn't get the client's business. I decided to treat all people the same whether they become clients or not. And to give clients the one thing I can offer for free when it's at all possible—my time and attention."

Needless to say, these were risky steps to take in the wake of a recession. Surely many of her friends and colleagues thought she was crazy. And Roberta admits that her first year was "lean to say the least." But her decision to focus on her areas of strength paid off in the long run. "On one of those early days when I actually had something to do an older man, without an appointment, knocked on my door and asked if I had time to speak with him. I put down my notes and invited him into my office. He was dressed like an average person but was carrying two bags with him. I listened for about an hour as he told me stories of his life and then near the end of our conversation he said, 'Oh, I bet you're wondering why I came in.' Then he lifted the bags onto my desk, gave me assets of several million dollars to manage for him and asked me to take care of him until he died. He still comes in once a week to have coffee and talk."

What Do You Have To Offer?

Think about your background, your processes, and your products or services. What is it that makes you special? Is it your efficiency, your ability to problem solve, your ability to quickly communicate, your understanding of technology, your innate ability to "read" other people? Whatever it is, you need to be able to identify it, explain it, embrace it and stick to it.

So how can you determine what your true strengths are? Ask yourself these questions:

- What natural abilities (public speaking, physical strength, big picture thinking, problem solving, rallying people to a cause, etc.) do I bring to the party?

- What knowledge and experience (years in a particular industry, years of study on a particular subject, etc.) do I possess that allows me to do what I do better than anyone else?

- What skills have I learned (sales techniques, building furniture, etc.) that allow me to use my knowledge and abilities consistently and to a high degree of success?

- What strengths do my customers tell me I have?

You're looking for the hard answers here, not the easy ones. If you're coming up with answers like, "I'm more passionate," "I have a stronger desire," "I work harder," or "My products are better," you're not focusing on the real reasons you're in business. You need to stop looking for things you can *claim* and start looking for the factual proof behind each claim. An easy way to do this is to follow the trail of whys. For example, if you answered, "My products are better," you could ask yourself, "*Why* are they better?" Then keep asking "Why?" until you discover the underlying natural ability, knowledge or skill that is at the root of your product's superiority.

Use the spaces below to write down your natural abilities, acquired knowledge and experience, and the skills you have that allow you to leverage those things. If you're having trouble coming up with answers, consider asking some close friends or even some ardent customers to help. Their objective opinions might be very enlightening.

My natural abilities are:

_____

_____

_____

_____

_____

My knowledge and experience includes:

_____

_____

_____

_____

_____

I have acquired the following skills:

_____

_____

_____

_____

_____

From my customers' perspective, my true
strengths are:

_____

_____

_____

_____

_____

Am I working to build and grow those strengths every day? If no, how can I start doing that today? If yes, what new directions could I explore?

_____

_____

_____

_____

_____

_____

_____

_____

_____

RULE 2

* * *

Make Reality Your Friend

"In the *New Normal*, the opportunities for success are plentiful. The trouble is, those opportunities are often different from the ones we are accustomed to. To exploit them, we have to think in new ways about ourselves and about the future."
— *Robert McNamee, author of* The New Normal

"Reality is the leading cause of stress amongst those in touch with it."
— *Jane Wagner*

If you believe the downturn in the economy is a temporary glitch, that life will one day soon bounce back to the way it was, and that your business will once again be able to run the way it used to—I'd like you to pour yourself a big strong cup of coffee and have a seat. This chapter is about seeing reality clearly and understanding what it means for your business. It's about embracing change, getting on with running your company and wooing your customers. It's about using your fear of change and uncertainty to fuel your future success. And it's about accepting things for what they are and making the capricious new world order work *for* you, not against you. There's a train coming. Following this rule will ensure that you're on that train, not under it. Ready? Here we go.

Change is happening at an exponential pace. Just think for a minute how much your own life has changed in the past 30 years or even the past five years! If you haven't adapted to the changes that have already occurred in the marketplace, you're going to find it incredibly difficult to woo customers for the future let alone to keep up with the onslaught of changes that are still on their way. If you've fallen behind, right now is the time to make adjustments to your business, your employees, your processes and even your product or service offerings to catch up with the current demands of the marketplace.

High Expectations Are Here To Stay

Anyone who has ever spent a day running a business would agree that customers' expectations aren't getting any easier to meet. Without question, the proliferation of technology and the integration of the web and all its advantages have created an ever more demanding, more educated and more discriminating customer. Today's customers come to your business insisting on higher quality, greater value and more efficiency than ever before. How can you deal with exponentially increasing customer demands?

The beautiful thing is that, as an entrepreneur, chances are good you are closer to your customers and much more in tune with their attitudes and behaviors than the average leader in a large corporation. Moreover, customer attitudes and behaviors can be surprisingly similar across industries, across products and services, and even across business-to-business and business-to-customer organizations. Put in simpler terms, we are all humans before we are customers and therefore the basics of what we demand from our service providers and product manufacturers remain the same. Which means wooing customers for the long term starts with an understanding of—and appreciation for—your own desires as a customer.

Years ago, I was working with a large client and listening to the leadership team as they vented their frustration about the heavy demands customers were placing on them. "They want us to deliver too quickly." "I don't know how they think we can produce this for the price they're asking!" You get the picture. They were counting on me to help them determine which of these expectations were simply too demanding for them to accept, to help them decide which of these customers were wrong for their business. I began by asking one simple question: "What are your customers demanding of you that you haven't asked for as a customer yourself?" At first I got a bunch of blank stares as everyone in the room took a minute to remember what it's like to be a customer. Then the light bulbs began to appear. The truth is, as a customer, you are demanding the same things—from your local grocery store, your dry cleaners, your favorite restaurant—that *your* customers are asking your business to provide: quality, efficiency, value and most of all, a commitment to keeping up with their changing needs.

Put your customer hat on.

- *As a customer, what expectations do you have when you spend money in your favorite stores?*
- *What about when you interact with a trusted service provider?*
- *How do the companies that meet your expectations do it?*
- *What about the ones that don't meet your expectations?*
- *What could* your *company learn from these examples?*

Not only does this constant escalation of customer expectations create the necessity for frequent process and product adjustments, but it also redefines the competitive landscape. Remember the good old days? You know, five or 10 years ago? It used to be easy to tell exactly who your competitors were. If you made a widget, your competition for customers was the widget maker just down the street. He was easy to identify because he was usually in the same local market, doing the same things you did. You kept an eye on his prices, his new product offerings, and his way of doing business. Maybe you even thought, "Hey, if I can copy these guys, do the same things they are doing but just a bit better, I'll win all the customers and keep them with us." Of course, that was back in the day when your biggest advertising spend was probably the local yellow pages or the local newspaper. Today, technology and instantly accessible information provide your customers with easy access to not only the products and services you offer but also every product and service offered by your competitors. Which means you have to begin thinking about your competition in a completely new way. Moreover, your competitors aren't who they used to be. Now, you are literally competing with the last best experience your customer had ... with *any* company.

Think about it. Today's customers are asking questions like, "Why can't the service at this restaurant be more like the online shoe store I ordered from last night? It would make my life so much easier!" I found myself doing this just the other day when I was searching for something on *Amazon*. I became frustrated when I put my mouse over the book title and it didn't automatically bring up a summary of the book. I realized that my expectation of the *Amazon* website (a bookstore, sort of) had not been met because my new benchmark for what type of functionality a website should have came from *Netflix*! On *Netflix.com,* when your cursor passes over a movie title or picture, a pop-up box instantly appears with a summary of the movie and its ratings as provided by other viewers. Now *Netflix* has nothing to do with selling books. And *Amazon* has nothing to do with renting movies. But my *expectation* of service for *any* online purchasing experience is now set because of my positive experience with *Netflix*. The bottom line is that your customers aren't making decisions about your product or service based solely on what your competition is doing. They are comparing your business to their most recent, most awesome buying experience. The best way to succeed in the modern competitive arena is to ask your customers what experiences are wowing them elsewhere and then look at ways to create a similar experience in your business. If you have developed a healthy dialogue with your customers, this will be remarkably easy to do. (You can read more about developing healthy dialogues in Rule 4.)

Put your customer hat on.

Think about your last best experience as a customer.

- *What did the company do to create a great experience for you?*
- *Are there other companies you'd like to see match that experience?*
- *Which companies do you think are creating new and positive expectations across industries?*

Respect The Power Of One

Another modern customer phenomenon you need to be on the lookout for is the all-powerful customer. Once again, easy access to the Internet and, frankly, the current trend of sharing our opinions on everything from what we had for breakfast to our latest interaction at a gas station, have given birth to a powerful and creative force that is affecting companies of every size. This makes perfect sense when you think about it. For more than a century, American corporations have held sway over the marketplace. Social networking has upset that balance and, while many a corporate leader might disagree, the change has been mostly for the good. Why? Because it roots out the providers who are dishonest or non-customer focused. Opinion aggregators and disseminators have proliferated. Today, a single consumer is able to tip the balance for or against your business in an instant. Individual customers have always had this power. (I have spent years talking about that one bad customer experience being shared with six other people.) But now customers can spread the word at, quite literally, light speed. Here's a great example of how one bad interaction can spread like wild fire.

"United Breaks Guitars"

In March 2008, David Carroll, a singer-songwriter from Canada was awaiting the departure of his *United Airlines*® flight at Chicago's O'Hare Airport when he was alerted by another passenger to look out the window. There he witnessed the baggage handlers *throwing* his band's guitars on the tarmac. Dave made several attempts to alert the crew who apparently demonstrated "complete indifference." I'm sure he got a response along the lines of, "Don't talk to me. Talk to the lead agent at your final destination." Upon arrival in Nebraska, his final destination, he was reunited with his $3,500 *Taylor*® guitar, which had a broken neck. Over the next year Dave tried, to no avail, to convince the airline to reimburse him for the $1,200 in repairs to his guitar but after dozens of communications the airline simply said no and closed his case. That's when Dave decided to take matters into his own hands. He created a song, performed it on video with his band and posted the video on *YouTube*®. Within one day the video had over 150,000 hits. By day three it had half a million hits. At the time of this writing Dave's video, "United Breaks Guitars" has been seen nearly 8 million times and Dave has been featured in *Time*® magazine and on *CNN*, *The View* and nearly all of the late night programs. The damage to the *United Airlines* brand was undeniable but perhaps the larger issue is what this lone customer's bad experience may have done to the bottom line. Chris Ayers of *Times Online*® estimates that the actual cash damage done to the airline was over $180 million dollars, or 10 percent of its market cap.[4] All because one guy was treated badly and decided to do something about it. Could your company afford that?

Beyond its entertainment value, there are so many important lessons that can be learned by entrepreneurs from this "power of one" story regarding customers. Former president of *SAS Airlines*® and customer loyalty pioneer Jan Carlzon calls every interaction you have with your customers—outbound marketing calls, inbound customer inquiries, online contacts, mail orders or face-to-face purchases—a "moment of truth."[5] In total, *United Airlines* personnel probably had dozens of these moments of truth with Dave Carroll—from the crew on his flight to the myriad employees he contacted over the phone and online. Each one of these interactions was an opportunity for a representative of the airline to listen, act and work toward a solution that would be meaningful to Dave and reasonable for the airline. In each of these moments, Carlzon notes, the company representative makes a *conscious* decision to create an advocate or create an angry customer who may decide to flex his or her "power of one" muscles. When every member of your organization understands that every single interaction with a customer is a "moment of truth" the process of wooing customers will actually begin.

Thanks to *YouTube, Yelp®, Twitter, Facebook®*, personal websites and blogs the Internet is loaded with opportunities for the individual customer to voice his or her opinion and either help or hurt a company. The power of one doesn't always have to be a negative. Just try Googling "i love virgin america" and you can begin to imagine the power of a single advocate as well. If you take the time to monitor these sites as an early warning system for your organization and explore ways to use them to spread positive word about your products or services, you will be way ahead in the race to woo customers and keep them coming back for more.

Take a minute right now to ask yourself if you're paying the right kind of attention to your online presence. Look beyond your website and the normal emails you receive in the course of doing business to what others may be saying about you online. Google has a wonderful free application that emails you daily alerts when your name or your company's name pops up on the web. It's a great way to see if the power of one is working in your favor. It also enables you to catch negative power-of-one comments early and deal with them before they become *YouTube* videos.

Time Is Where The Money Is

I actually found myself tapping my foot the other day during the five seconds it took for my bank's ATM to print my receipt. In the words of actress and bestselling author Carrie Fisher, "Instant gratification takes too long." Remember when you had to go all the way *into* the bank to get cash from your account? Remember when you had to wait for a check or invoice to arrive via (gasp) regular mail? Well those times are over my friend. Today, patience is in short supply and time is *more* valuable than money.

I think we can all agree that life, for customers, is so much easier than it was years ago. Today you can sign up for a new service or switch providers with the click of a mouse. And that ease-of-use, that timesaving click, has become valuable in its own right. Because, as customers, we've become willing to *pay extra* when a company gives us the opportunity to save time and effort. In other words, trying to compete on price is archaic at best and suicidal at worst. Why? First of all, customers who make purchase decisions based solely on price are, by their very definition, not going to be "woo-able" for the long term. Their loyalty has already been given to the almighty dollar or 23 cents or however much they can keep out of your till and in their own pockets. Sure, you could win them over today with a bargain. But tomorrow they'll be snuggling up to your competitor just because she dropped her price by a few pennies. The good news is, if you can create processes that save customers time, enable them to interact with you with ease, or demonstrate how much you value their time you will bind customers to you for a reason greater than money. And you will make it difficult for them to leave you for somebody else.

The transportation company I use to get back and forth to the airport is a great example. They save me time and they make my life easy. They know that I always want them to arrive 10 minutes early in case I'm ready to go ahead of time. They also know that I cut things really close. And they know I like to be dropped off at a certain place at the airport because the security lines are shorter there. This company has bound me to them by making things fast and easy for me. If I were to go to another car service to save money it would be a major hassle. It might cost me less but switching would use up a great deal of my time because I would have to teach the new company about my preferences. I can get more money. What I can't get more of, what is in shortest supply, is time.

There's a whole category of service plans designed around our willingness to pay for the opportunity to save time. They're called "pay for service" plans and they usually have a couple of levels. With "gold level" service you are given the privilege of not having to wait in a queue when you call the 800 number for assistance. You're connected immediately with an intelligent human being who is equipped to resolve your issue. A number of airlines now let you pay extra to use the premier flyer line at the ticket counter so you don't have to wait in the long line of leisure travelers. *American Express Platinum* costs extra but it means you get instant access to a capable person who can resolve product issues, make dinner reservations or purchase a gift for someone 24/7. That has value for me. What has value for your customers?

Here's a great example. The other day my computer server died. I had paid extra for a premium level service plan when I bought the server, so I got on the phone and within two hours the installers were at my office with a new server. That's great service. I paid for it but I was happy to do so. Why? Because it saved me time. Think about a business you frequent, not because of their price but because of the time they save you. Now think about your business. Do you have processes in place that demonstrate how much you value your customers' time?

The bottom line is, you don't want to compete on price. Trying to compete on price is a losing battle because someone will always undercut you until you are unable to sustain a profitable business model. If you want to go out of business, design your business model around being the lowest-cost provider. If you want to be successful for years to come, design your business model around the currency of time.

> ### Put your customer hat on.
>
> Think of the product and service providers in your life that make things readily accessible, quick and easy to use.
>
> - *Are you willing to pay a little more for that consistent, easy experience?*
> - *What do they do to make your interaction with them effortless?*
> - *Does that effortlessness help keep you loyal?*

Technology Might Not Save You

As I travel around the country speaking about service, one of the questions I love asking from the podium is, "How many of you work *around* the technology in your company every day to serve your clients?" Almost without exception, regardless of industry, at least 80 percent of the room will raise their hands. Believe it or not (and some days I don't believe it!), technology is actually supposed to help you be more effective, efficient and ideally provide better service to your customers. But electronic systems, high-tech devices and fancy software programs are not necessarily going to provide you with all of that. Despite all of the technological advances that have come to pass—and will come to pass—you still need to use your brain. You need to choose your technological solutions

> "Technology just helps us do stupid things ... faster"
>
> — *Kevin Kelly, Founder of Wired Magazine*

carefully and use them judiciously. The truth is, many of us have spent years adapting to technology rather than requiring it to adapt to us. We've gotten comfortable with the hurdles and no longer see how they impede our progress. If you are serious about attracting loyal customers, take a good look around your business, chat with your front line employees, query a few customers and find out if your technology is helping or hurting your business. If it's not making you better, faster and smarter at what you do, eliminate it until something comes along that does.

Pacific Specialty Insurance Company

I recently had the experience of purchasing a new scooter—yes, I said scooter—for errands around town and basic transportation in the land of no parking, otherwise known as San Francisco. I purchased my scooter from a friend who recommended the insurance company she had used for her scooter coverage. So I visited the company's website to apply. After navigating for what seemed like an eternity, I was unable to find an online application portal or even a phone number that I could call to apply over the phone.

Luckily, my friend provided me with a reference bill that had a phone number on it. So I called that number and got through to a call center somewhere apparently in the Himalayas. I told the call center representative that I would like to buy some insurance for my new scooter. And I explained that I thought it might be a fairly easy process as they had carried the insurance on this same scooter for the previous owner. After a series of questions around the VIN number

(25 digits) the serial number (14 digits) the make, model, etc., I finally asked if they didn't already have this information. "We do," the woman replied, "but we can't see it on our screens. That's a different system than ours. We can only see the name and the billing information."

Okay, I thought. I get it ... different systems. I would normally have hung up but I had already invested 15 minutes of my time just getting to this point so I thought I would give them a break and continue with the process. As the questions continued, I asked if there was some place online I could enter this information and the woman said, "Yeah, I think so but don't know where it is so we might as well keep going." Well, okay ... *we* might as well. Finally, after giving every piece of data including my blood type to this gal, she gave me a quote that was *three times* the rate on my friend's bill. I explained this and we went back through the information to understand the source of the discrepancy. Finally, after another painful few minutes, we discovered that the reason the quote was higher was that my mileage was expected to be higher. No, I said, it will be the same—approximately 500 miles per year. We went through the process again with the same result. Then the woman realized that the computer system wouldn't let her enter such a low number of miles. The lowest it would go was 4,900 miles per year. Silence.

Now, San Francisco is a city that is seven miles long by seven miles wide. I'd have to ride my scooter 20 hours a day to travel 4,900 miles in a year! She told me the only way around this was for her to mail me an application. (She couldn't email it because they were not allowed to use the Internet.) I could fill out the printed application and send it back to them with my check and *then* I might get the insurance. It took me four weeks, five mail communications and numerous phone calls to finally get coverage. When I received my final contract document in the mail, what do you think was written in the "annual miles driven" column? That's right, 4,900 miles.

With the proliferation of off-the-shelf, low-cost technology available for everything from customer management systems to invoicing to procurement to production systems, there is simply no excuse for a business of any size to work *around* technology. If you are of a "certain age" and you didn't grow up with technology, do yourself a favor and hire someone under 30 years old to research the best tools for your business and make a recommendation. If you think you can't afford it, think about how much the lack of efficient technology will cost you, your employees and your business if your customers leave you for someone with a better system. If your technology isn't helping you serve customers faster, more cost efficiently or with a higher level of service, change it or get rid of it!

Second Chances Are Earned

You have a favorite restaurant, don't you? A place you go where they're always happy to see you again. Where they seat you at your favorite table, the experience is nice and the food is predictable and consistent. Most people's favorite restaurants aren't expensive five-star establishments. They're more often dependable and consistent neighborhood bistros. Now let me ask you this. What happens if, one night, you go to your favorite restaurant and have an "off" experience? Let's say, the food comes out cold or you get the wrong salad or maybe the server is short with you. Whatever the details it's an odd or somehow mediocre experience. As you leave the restaurant or bistro or McDonald's or whatever, do you hop in your car, turn to your dinner partner and say, "Gosh that was weird" and then go back another night and give them another chance? I'm betting you would. Because when you stack that one bad experience up against all the positive experiences you've had there, that "off" night feels like an anomaly. Right? So now, what happens if that was your *first visit* to that restaurant? Would you go back and give them another chance? Probably not. More than likely, you would tell all your friends not to frequent that establishment. One of the greatest gifts that truly wooing your customers can give your business is the opportunity for second chances. Strong customer relationships allow you to build a resilient business that can survive a missed deadline, an issue with quality or just an "off" day.

Sincerity Is The New Black

I know. You thought 40 was the new black. Or wait, 40 is the new 30. That's right. Anyway, my point is, sincerity is the new black. It's the über-essential that any modern entrepreneur needs in his or her collection of business success secrets. I think probably we can place the blame for this squarely on the shoulders of Generation Y. Why? Well, because Gen Y demands authenticity, honesty and transparency. When members of this generation feel you aren't being straightforward and honest they make it their mission to avoid working with you. Actually, we can't really blame one generation for making sincerity so critical in the marketplace. For the most part, all customers are beginning to expect that you treat them with sincerity. And that's really a good thing. Because, as your couples therapists have all told you, a healthy relationship is one that is based on trust.

Now let's talk about your local chain grocery store for a minute. (I know it feels like I'm jumping around but it'll all come together in the end, I promise.) At your local grocery store, your receipt has your name printed on it. And at the end of your transaction, the cashier dutifully reads the receipt and says, "Thank you Mrs. So-And-So" or "Thank you Mr. Such-And-Such." In my experience the cashiers usually don't even look at you when they perform this feat of customer service. They're just going through the motions.

I could be wrong but I'm guessing some overly enthusiastic former salesman of the year—the type that uses your name repeatedly in a conversation in an effort to endear himself to you—told the chief executives of all the big chain grocery stores in our country that people form relationships with you when you use their names. (Recent studies have shown that touching someone makes them more inclined toward you as well, but let's not go there shall we?) But using your name à la carte—just performing the task perfunctorily without the accompaniment of sincerity—doesn't endear you to those grocery cashiers at all, does it? As a matter of fact, when performed without feeling, calling you by name does the exact opposite of what it's intended to do. It feels like a stranger is getting too personal, which is just plain annoying.

How many companies these days are making the mistake of putting policies in place that require actions that lack sincerity? When you call an 800 number and fail to get resolution or even an apology for your issue, why does the person on the other end of the line finish the call with, "Is there anything else I can help you with today?" Then you say, "Yes you can solve the problem I called about." And they say, "I'm sorry I can't do that. Is there anything *else* I can help you with today?"

That line was put in the customer service script in an effort to please customers but, without sincerity, it becomes a maddening and vicious loop of not getting your needs met. Wooing customers can't be scripted. Successfully wooing customers requires employees who can think on their feet. Caring human beings who are genuine and authentic and passionate about the purchasing public. People who have been given a framework for decision making that allows them to find a solution to a customer's issue during that moment of truth. You don't have to know my name or provide me with five-star service to gain my loyalty. But you do have to look me in the eye, make me feel like you appreciate my being there and give me the firm impression that you hope I will come back. That's what will woo me.

What's The Reality Of Your Business?

Take time now to ask yourself these questions:

- What are the current expectations for my industry?

- What new expectations for other industries might affect my business?

- What expectations have my competitors set that I need to adjust to?

- What easy service experiences have I had? Are there elements of that experience I can apply to my own business?

- How am I monitoring changing expectations? (In person, online, etc.)

- What opportunities do I have to use "the power of one" to promote my business? Am I helping my most loyal customers spread the word about my business? What more could I do?

- What "hoops" do my customers have to jump through to work efficiently with me? Am I using technology to help my employees better serve customers?

- Have I stood in my customers' shoes when it comes to dealing with me and my company? What are my service touch points that could be improved upon?

- How can I save customers more time? How can I show them I value their time?

- Could I offer a premium level service that expedites things for customers who are willing to pay for the time savings?

- What devices and/or systems do I need to get rid of, reprogram or alter to make them work for me not against me?

- What devices and/or systems do I have that I am not using or not using properly? Are there any new technological advances that could help me run my business more efficiently?

- How am I demonstrating sincerity in my dealings with customers? What "scripted" elements to my service could be changed to allow employees to engage at a more sincere level with my customers?

- What additional autonomy do I need to give my employees to enable them to more effectively and efficiently deal with customers? What more could I do?

- Do I need to eliminate any perfunctory duties that are creating an environment of insincerity?

RULE 3

* * *

Zero In On Your Target

If you're going to hunt elephants, don't get off the trail for a rabbit.
— *T. Boone Pickens*

Not long ago a friend of mine who lives in a ski resort town walked into her local grocery store to pick up some things for dinner. At the entrance of the store, next to the shopping cart corral, was a man sitting at a table with copies of the local newspaper on it. Each time someone with a heartbeat walked through the front doors he shouted at them, "MA'AM! ARE YOU LOCAL? DO YOU GET THE PAPER DELIVERED?!" When my friend responded that she had an online subscription to a different paper the man proceeded to berate her for not choosing to have his paper physically delivered.

Now there are a lot of things wrong with this picture, the first being that probably 90 percent of the people shopping in that store were from another state or even another country. But the main point is this particular newspaper company was so desperate for customers they had decided *anybody* would do and *any tactics* were valid. This scenario is not unlike a single person standing on a busy street corner shouting dinner invitations at everyone who drives by and berating those who decline or say they are already taken. How successful do you think that newspaper publisher was at winning new customers? If you guessed "not very," you're probably right.

Choosing Everybody Is Choosing Nobody

Too many entrepreneurs make the mistake of believing that *everyone* is a potential customer. I am begging you right now *not* to be one of them. Everyone really means no one in particular. Choosing to target everyone is just plain lazy. And frankly, going after the wrong person for the wrong reasons in any scenario is just plain depressing. Just as you aren't a potential customer for every Tom, Dick, Harry & Co. out there, neither is everyone a potential customer of yours. If I'm not inclined toward your particular business, you can market to me all day long and no matter what you say, how cheaply you sell it, how easy you make it ... I'll never buy it.

To woo your ideal customers properly and thereby win their loyalty for the long term you must first fully understand who they are, what their needs are, what their expectations are and most importantly ... whether or not you can fulfill those needs and expectations. Finding the right customers for your business is the key to *profitable* sales, *steady* growth and long-term viability. Once you have thought about and defined your true strengths as a company, deciding who fits you best is remarkably easy.

So who are your best customers? I don't mean who spends the most money with you. I mean who does it feel easy to serve? Who seems to have an understanding of what you do? Who has a need that is fulfilled by your business? Who inspires you to say, "Gosh, if I only had a million customers like him or her, I'd have it made!" Most likely those folks are your best customers for a reason.

The alignment of a customer's needs and expectations with the strengths of your organization is what creates that magical synchronicity that makes some people easier to serve than others. I'm willing to bet you have customers who spend a great deal of money with you but each interaction with them is a horrible experience. Not because they are bad people (well, frankly some may be) but because they are trying to get you to fulfill a need that your product or service isn't designed to fill. Other customers are a joy to serve from the moment they first walk through your door.

Put your customer hat on.

- *Are there places you shop where your transactions just seem easier?*

- *What defines "easier" for you? And, what do they do to create that experience?*

- *Are there other businesses that make you feel uncomfortable every time you go in? Is it because your needs don't really get fulfilled there?*

Manage Your BFFs and Frenemies

About two percent of your customers are what I call *Diehard Advocates*. They're your BFFs (best friends forever). They love you and your product or service so much that they talk about you all the time. They recommend you to friends and neighbors; they simply can't get enough of you. They share their stories of how they found you and why everyone should buy from you, work with you, partner with you. These include your mother, and your best friends, among others. They fit perfectly with you because they need exactly what your company provides. And you love them too. So much so that you spend a lot of time with them when they come by. But be warned, spending too much time with these folks can fool you into making broad assumptions about your whole customer base, assumptions that can get you into trouble. (More about that later.)

The greatest gift of the *Diehard Advocates* is something that many entrepreneurs overlook. These folks talk about you without being asked. Just imagine what they could do for you if you could direct their advocacy toward your untapped prospects. This is what social media can do for your company. And it doesn't have to cost you a dime. *Yelp*, *Facebook* and myriad other opinion aggregators are at your disposal. Just ask your advocates to write a review for you. "Got something great to say about us? Put it on *LinkedIn* or on your own blog. We'd love it if you could help others find us!" Advocates already want to help you. So let them! Ask them to serve as references or even to write you a recommendation letter. Ask them to directly connect you to others who might be interested in your product or service. You can even give them a discount or a gift for their effort but you don't have to ... *Diehard Advocates* just like to help!

Another two percent of your customers are at the other end of the spectrum. This is the group of customers I affectionately call *Serial Killers.* The ones whose calls you let go to voicemail because you simply can't "deal with them today." Each time one of them enters your store, office or restaurant you get that familiar sinking feeling in your stomach. The feeling that tells you no matter what you do, no matter how hard you try, nothing in the world will make this person happy. You can package your products in a different color. You can sell them in twos instead of threes. You can assign your best sales person or account manager. You can deliver your products faster, cheaper and with a bow on top. And it still doesn't matter. The *Serial Killer* is displeased. The *Serial Killer* wants to speak to the owner.

A few years ago one of my clients had a *Serial Killer* that had been plaguing their leadership team for years. They had done literally hundreds of customized jobs for this customer. He was considered a real moneymaker whom they didn't want to lose. I happened to be there one day when this customer was scheduled to come in for a meeting so I decided to try a little experiment. I asked the team to keep track of how much time they spent with this customer. How much money they knocked off the price. How much the customizations cost and, most importantly, how much time they spent after the sale trying to make/keep this customer happy. At the end of a month, they determined that their *Serial Killer* was costing them five times as much to serve as their average customer. They were actually *losing* money every time this person bought from them.

These are the folks that remind you the customer *isn't* always right. They're definitely not right for you. They will kill you with their demands and then turn around and tell all of their friends and colleagues how terrible you are. The best and only way to remedy the situation is to put your arm lovingly around your *Serial Killers'* shoulders and walk them directly to your competition. They'll suck the life out of your competitors. But hey, better them than you.

Put your customer hat on.

- *For whom are you a* Diehard Advocate?
- *What is it that they do for you that makes you an advocate?*
- *What would you be willing to do for them?*
- *Which companies do you patronize steadily and quietly without getting too involved?*
- *What would those companies need to do to move you to advocacy?*

Spend Time Wooing The Worthy

In between these two extremes are the 96 percent of your customers on whom you should focus most of your time because they are your bread and butter: the *Steady Eddies*. These are the quiet ones who don't raise their hands or a ruckus but just calmly give you their money day in and day out. These are the customers that you never think much about ... until one day when you look around and find they aren't there anymore. They've quietly taken their money somewhere else. How much money? Let me put it this way ... could you afford to lose 96 cents of every dollar you make? I thought not.

Making time for this important segment of your customers is not only good business it is also absolutely essential to your survival. As we learned in the introduction to this book, mere satisfaction isn't enough to keep people coming back time and time again. In fact, it's downright boring. To ensure lasting success, you have to create a deeper, more meaningful relationship with those customers who are the backbone of your business. Sure, communicating with the *Steady Eddies* may be more challenging. They believe they already know you well enough and they assume you know enough about them. But a bond based on assumptions can be easily broken. If you don't pursue a deeper relationship, your *Steady Eddies* may surrender to the advances of your competitors.

If you look closely at your own behavior as a customer—the demands you place upon those who sell you products and services—you can begin to appreciate what you have to do in order to meet your *Steady Eddies'* needs. Think about the things you purchase day in and day out from providers you aren't really "loyal" to yet. The ones that you wouldn't hesitate to cheat on if you had to go out of your way to get to them or if you found another similar product that was less expensive. These companies seem to be satisfying your immediate needs but they aren't really wooing you, are they? What if one of these companies reached out to you one day in an effort to find a new, faster, or better way to serve you? What if this company started to build a relationship with you that made you begin to really care about their success? As a business owner, that's your sweet spot.

By reaching out to your *Steady Eddies* and learning more about them and their needs you will begin to develop a real connection with them and you may even succeed in creating more advocates for your business. Just as in any relationship, the more work you put into it, the more you will get out of it ... and the more likely the relationship is to last. Think of how easy it would be for you to get to know your customers better. Do you know which of your *Steady Eddies* could be moved to *Diehard Advocates*? What would it take? Here's a great story that illustrates the reason *Steady Eddies* fly the coop.

Taken To The Cleaners

There is a local dry cleaner I patronized for a couple of years. It's a small mom-and-pop operation that I chose specifically because I like to support local entrepreneurs. Because of my speaking and training work, I travel a great deal and I do a lot of dry cleaning. So naturally I was in this shop at least once, if not twice, a week and had been for years. I had to be one of their very best customers. Every time I went in there, the same woman was behind the register and we went through the same routine. I would put my armful of clothes on the counter and she would look me dead in the eye and say, "Name, please."

One day, I was feeling a bit crabby so I looked right back at her and said, "Guess."

After an uncomfortable pause she said, "Solomon."

I said, "Right."

She said, "Okay." She wrote it down. Then she said, "How much starch?"

"Guess."

"Medium."

"Right." (She still didn't get the game.)

Next she says, "Phone number."

I said, "Ooh, this is a tough one. But guess."

Believe it or not, she had my phone number memorized. She wrote it down. Now, at this point, I was very pleased with myself. I felt as though we'd had a breakthrough, that we had an unspoken understanding. I walked away with my clean clothes feeling as though we'd reached a new level in our relationship. Three days later I went back in with some additional items. I walked up to the counter. She looked me dead in the eye and said, "Name, please." I just stared at her, dumbfounded. I couldn't believe it. It was clear that she remembered me. It was clear she had all the information. But she made a choice not to act on it.

I got something in the mail shortly after that experience that advertised the opening of a new dry cleaner about two miles from my house. Not really very convenient. The hours actually weren't as good. And it was more expensive. But you know what? I was probably their first customer. Did I ever go back to my local dry cleaner and share with her that, to keep me as a customer, all she had to do was acknowledge the amount of time and money I spent with her? That all she had to do was recognize and respect me? No. A friend of mine says the worst possible thing you can do to a company is not complain because they'll never know what they're doing wrong and have the opportunity to fix it.

So what have we learned? My dry cleaner knew I was a good customer but she chose not to build a relationship with me. How many of your customers do you treat the same way? If you don't hear from them they must be just fine right? Remember, these customers are the most important people to your business. It is absolutely essential to the future of your business that you find a way to acknowledge and show appreciation for your *Steady Eddies* or, as I did, they will take their money to your competition. Starting that dialogue can be as simple as remembering someone's name.

Put your customer hat on.

- *Who recognizes you by name?*
- *Who treats you like they know you even if they don't remember your name?*
- *How do they do it?*
- *How do you feel about them?*
- *Does that keep you loyal to them?*
- *What more would they have to do to increase your loyalty to them?*
- *What actions on their part would cause you to interact with them more frequently?*

Keep An Eye On The Exit

Think about a time when you decided to stop patronizing a particular store or supplier. Did you use the simplest and least confrontational way to end the relationship—that all encompassing but non-personal catch-all of price? Does this sound familiar, "No really, it's nothing you've done. We simply found a better price elsewhere." As an entrepreneur, you've probably heard this a thousand times. As a consumer you've probably *used* it a thousand times ... and for good reason. The price catchall allows both parties to save face and avoid further dialogue that might get, well, difficult. But what's the reality behind these "price" departures? How often is price really the issue?

Not often, in fact. The sad truth is that only about nine percent of customers who leave citing price as their main reason for departing are really telling the truth. Years ago, *The American Society of Quality Control* conducted a study to determine why customers leave a company.[6] The individual reasons might seem inconsequential upon first view. However, taken as a whole, they can offer useful insight into the relationship between your business and your customers. What were some of the real reasons these customers left?

1. Customer was turned away by the indifferent attitude of a company employee (68 percent)
2. Customer was dissatisfied with the product (14 percent)

3. Customer was lured away by competition (nine percent)
4. Customer was influenced by a friend to go elsewhere (five percent)
5. Customer moves away or dies (four percent)

Regardless of the reasons, we've all had those conversations both as customers and as owners.

WHAT WE SAY...

Owner: We're so sorry to see you go! We've valued your business over the years.

Customer: *Oh well, we've enjoyed working with you too but we got a much better offer from another vendor.*

Owner: We'd love to see if we could match that price for you...

Customer: *That's so nice of you but it's a great price and we've already started to make the move. Great working with you. Bye!*

WHAT WE MEAN...

Owner: Ack! What do you mean you are leaving? Just like that? You never said anything before! I had no idea you weren't happy! I'm going to *strangle* your account manager!

Customer: *Geez, I guess it takes my leaving for you to spend even five minutes on the phone with me!*

> *If you had let me know how much you valued*
> *my business over the past three years, I might*
> *have considered staying with you. Frankly,*
> *moving elsewhere is a real pain.*

Owner: Seriously, what can I do to keep you? What
            if I undercut their price by 10 percent?

Customer: *Sorry, shmuck. Too little, too late. And by the*
            way, your processes stink!

Owner: My processes? What do you mean? Hey! Come
            back here!

One of the best things you can do for your business today is take a look at the customers who have left you and spend some time figuring out why they really left. If you've got a database that breaks out customers who haven't ordered from you in a while, or who used you once and never came back, try reaching out to them. Hire a third party from outside your organization to talk with these former customers and see if they would be willing to help you create a better experience for your customers. You can do this very inexpensively by using an intern from your local college or, better yet, look on websites such as *www.elance.com* for someone who specializes in interviewing people. You'll be pleasantly surprised by how many former customers are happy and even honored to offer their opinions and advice on polishing your business processes. Who knows, some of them may even give you another chance!

Put your customer hat on.

Think about the last product or service provider you left.

- *Was it really because of price or was there "more" that you didn't tell them?*
- *If you were asked to provide advice for a business you stopped using, would you help?*
- *Maybe even feel a little flattered?*
- *What would they need to do for you in return for your help?*

The questions you need to ask to get to the heart of why your *Steady Eddies* leave will differ depending on your company and type of product or service but here are some rules of thumb you can think about as you design your questionnaire:

1. *Give Them Space*—Make sure to explain upfront that this is a third party survey seeking to help XYZ company better serve its current and future customers. People love to help and if they are really dissatisfied with something, it gives them an opportunity to vent to you rather than to all of their friends.

2. *Keep It Informal*—Don't ask a million questions or "on a scale of one to five" type questions. Just hold an honest, structured conversation. Remember,

unlike a more formal customer loyalty questionnaire, this is really only trying to answer one question, "What could XYZ company have done to keep your business?"

3. *Behavioral Data Is Best*—Make sure the data you are getting is actionable by ensuring your questions are focused on specific behaviors, elements of service, quality, etc. For example, "If you could change anything about how XYZ provides its products or services, what would that be?" or "What specifically could XYZ company have done to make the buying process easier for you?"

4. *Ask For Anything Else*—Always close the interview with one more chance for customers to "come clean" if they haven't up to that point. For example, "Is there anything else you would like me to know about your experience with XYZ company?" Sometimes people have difficulty sharing their thoughts unless you ask about them directly. If you haven't touched on the topic that is important to them before now, this gives you one last chance to allow them to open up.

Who's Really Worth Wooing?

- Who are my *Diehard Advocates*? Am I asking them to "channel" their positive feedback to others? How can I make that process easy for them?

- Who are my top 20 *Steady Eddies* and how can I create a deeper and more proactive dialogue between them and my company? How can I help move them to advocacy?

- How much are my most difficult customers really costing me in time, effort and customization? When I look at their true profitability, are they worth it? Can I better set their expectations to ensure loyalty or are they "un-woo-able?" If they aren't worth keeping, how can I help them move to another company that might better meet their needs?

- Can I create a dialogue with customers who have left me after only one purchase or switched to a competitor? How can I initiate a simple and honest conversation with them to help inform my future interactions?

RULE 4

* * *

Commit To A True Dialogue

"A conversation is a dialogue, not a monologue. That's
why there are so few good conversations: due to
scarcity, two intelligent talkers seldom meet."
— *Truman Capote*

"A dialogue is more than two monologues."
— *Max Kampelman*

As business owners, we have been taught that if we
consistently direct our communications *out* to customers we will build their awareness of our companies and
therefore increase sales. We reinforce these beliefs with
the now ubiquitous brand awareness studies that offer
us "proof" of our popularity. Over the past 30 years,
however, that one-way communication process has been
bearing less and less fruit. We place ads, send emails,
post web pages, and push information out. But the

competition for consumers' attention is fierce and mere awareness is no longer enough to convince people to try our products or services, let alone commit to them for the long haul.

Today, successfully wooing loyal customers requires that you create real opportunities for the open exchange of ideas between those individuals and your business. Establishing and maintaining a true dialogue allows learning to occur on *both* sides of the conversation. You learn about your customers' values, beliefs and needs. At the same time, they better understand how your strengths can benefit them. Creating this sort of open exchange might seem like a simple task. The truth is, it takes a concerted effort that resonates through your organization and permeates everything you do.

Roberta Winchell, the attorney we met in the first chapter who broke legal industry protocol by giving her time and attention to people freely, understands the meaning of true dialogue. She begins each client relationship by listening carefully to her clients' issues off the clock. Then, instead of rushing into selling them a solution, she takes time to teach them about the legal processes involved in resolving their particular issue. Other law firms might consider this risky behavior because she is essentially giving away her expertise for free. But Roberta's experience has proven the opposite to be true. "I allow them to leave without feeling pressured to make a decision," she says, "and they reward me by not only returning as active clients but also becoming supportive advocates for my business."

Stop Making Assumptions

The first step in creating business processes that allow true dialogue is eliminating the common practice of making broad assumptions about your customers. Renowned interior and product designer Angelo Donghia put it best when he said, "Assumption is the mother of the screw up." Deny it if you wish, but the truth is, we all like to think we know our customers inside and out. As an entrepreneur you probably pride yourself in talking with your customers on a regular basis. Unfortunately this sort of unscientific research can lead you to make assumptions about the *many* based on the *few*. Chances are good that most of the customers you interact with fall into the *Serial Killer* and *Diehard Advocate* categories we spoke of earlier. Remember, those are only about four percent of your customer base. Yet how many times have you, unconsciously or otherwise, formed a global opinion about *all* of your customers as a result of those interactions? How often have you changed a business practice to accommodate a *Serial Killer* or a *Diehard Advocate* without consulting your *Steady Eddies*?

> "We focus on preselected segments of the seen and generalize it to be the unseen; the error of confirmation."
>
> —*Nassim Nicholas Taleb,*
> *author of* The Black Swan

Once you have a set of assumptions collected from your most extroverted customers you, consciously or not, spend your conversations with everybody else seeking to confirm what you believe to be true. *"See? He loves the new salsa! Everybody loves the new salsa."* This behavior is extremely common and also extremely dangerous as it moves your business farther and farther away from the *Steady Eddies*, who can help you discern the truth about your current operation and your most promising areas for growth. Even if you make a concerted effort to talk regularly with a wider selection of your customers, are you doing it in a consistent and unbiased way? Moreover, are your "research subjects" telling you what they know or what they think you want to hear? Keen observation of your customers' attitudes and behaviors is important. But observation can only tell you so much. To get to the meat of what your customers want and need from your business—to get the information you need to properly woo your *Steady Eddies* into a more meaningful connection with your business.

> "My customers don't have time for surveys. They're busy people. The last thing I want to do is scare/burden/annoy them with a bunch of questions."
>
> —*You*

You probably have ten thousand number one priorities on any given day but this *Rule of Woo* is vitally important to your long-term profitability. If you can focus on creating a true dialogue, getting the real data and identifying the real areas of opportunity with your *Steady Eddies* you can leave your competition in the dust. The truth is your customers *want* to be more involved in your business. They have opinions they're dying to share with you. After all, they're in a partnership with you. They need you to be successful because the better you serve them, the more effectively and efficiently you meet their needs, the more value they get out of the deal. Asking them to share their honest opinions about your business shows that you have respect for their time, their money and their partnership in your success.

Think about your own needs as a consumer for a minute. Doesn't your life get easier if you can deal with companies you know and trust? Companies that value you and your business so much that they work hard to provide you with better and better service and consistently meet your expectations? In today's crazy world that kind of predictability is a wonderful thing!

Start The Conversation

Once you've cleansed yourself of your assumptions, you're ready to initiate a conversation and establish an open exchange of ideas with your customers. As we discussed earlier, those *Steady Eddies* aren't going to give you any information without your going out and actively seeking it. Proactive interaction with your core customers will help you discern their true likes, dislikes, hot buttons and more. But any old interaction won't do. Getting to know your customers requires asking the right questions in a nonthreatening environment, listening to their answers with an open mind, *and acting on* their responses in a way that improves their experience with your business.

Use Your Listening Posts

One of the easiest and most cost-effective ways to keep tabs on customer mindsets and identify trends is to make use of "listening posts" that already exist within your organization. Your listening posts are your delivery people, your receptionist, your part timers and even your accounts receivable personnel—the individuals within your organization who interact with your *Steady Eddies* every day. Creating a formal way of collecting insights from these people on a monthly, weekly or daily basis will enable you to better understand your customers and, more importantly, identify trends that might not turn up until survey time. These gatherings can range from quick ten-minute huddles at the beginning of each shift to more formal sit-down meetings with larger teams. When provided with regular opportunities to share their customer insights with the rest of the team, your listening posts can offer an enormously expedient way to keep your finger on the pulse of your customer base.

> *"I keep hearing parents talking about how long it takes them to get ready to ski with their kids."*
> (Hmm, how would we help parents with kids get from the car to the lifts faster?)

> *"This man said his other grocery store gives him a code so he can trace the origins of the food he's buying."*
> (Wow. Maybe we should look into providing that service too.)

Talk To The Right People

One place where technology has really given us a leg up is in our ability to keep track of our customers and find innovative ways to gather their opinions. Putting together a meaningful customer loyalty study no longer requires fancy consultants, paper and pencil surveys and monster databases. However, it does require that you and your team create questions that are actionable. By this, I mean questions that will help you define and grow your strengths, identify problem areas, seek out new opportunities and deepen the involvement of your customers in your business, thereby deepening their loyalty to you. There are as many ways to collect and manage customer information as there are companies but here are some basic guidelines and recommendations for how to build and execute a great customer loyalty study. And I do mean *loyalty*. Remember, measuring satisfaction doesn't help you woo anyone. You have to get at the heart of what creates true loyalty or you've wasted your efforts.

If you've got a customer database that includes email addresses, congratulations! For most business-to-business companies, this is a no brainer. You'll want to survey your top 40 percent of customers based on revenue. Ideally, you're choosing 20 percent of those who are your biggest revenue generators as well as 20 percent that you know could be bigger but aren't. Remember, people want to help you succeed and they love to give you their opinions.

For those of you who don't have easy access to your customers' contact information don't despair. There are plenty of creative ways to get their contact information and solicit their opinions about your business:

- Ski resorts pass out postcards offering a free coffee or a discount on a lift ticket if you sign into their web-based survey.

- A restaurant gives a free appetizer on your next visit if you fill out their online survey and/or provide your email so they can send you one.
- A local bakery/coffee shop provides a free coffee for your completed survey.
- A child care center provides weekly email photos of your child at play if you sit on their parent advisory email panel and offer ongoing feedback on how they can improve their service.
- You can institute a "customer loyalty" program in which you offer a discount or other incentive in exchange for opinions and information.
- Believe it or not, those silly business card drops for a prize still work like a charm!

Sometimes it doesn't even take a database to get your customers communicating with you on an ongoing daily, or even minute-by-minute, basis. Here's a really terrific story about how Mt. Hood Meadows *(www.skihood.com)* Ski Resort used a negative issue (erratic weather patterns) to create an open dialogue that actually grew their business and secured the loyalty of their customers.

Mt. Hood Meadows
If you think your business has difficult variables to manage try running a ski resort in one of the most volatile weather climates in the country. Dealing with the effects of snowstorms and high winds are an integral part of any ski area's operation. But Mt. Hood, just outside of Portland, Oregon, has exceptional

challenges as their weather is driven by the maritime climate of the Northwest. In this unpredictable climate, gale-force winds and erratic freezing levels can force ski lift closures with little or no advance warning, as the towers can accumulate several inches of ice in a matter of minutes. These sudden operational interruptions create disappointed and sometimes angry guests, particularly if those guests don't learn about a lift closure until they have already made the hour-and-a-half trek from Portland.

During the 2008–2009 winter season, a series of such weather-related incidents generated an unusually high number of negative guest comments. While the Mt. Hood Meadows leadership team knew they couldn't control the weather they decided they *could* control the expectations of their guests by improving their communications about the weather and how it was affecting the lifts. During the summer between seasons, Mt. Hood's leaders created a new guest service strategy that was dubbed the "855 Program". This program put processes in place that enabled the resort to open their base lifts without fail at 8:55 a.m.—five minutes before the published opening time—every day of the season. It also established new communications procedures that allowed the resort to communicate honestly and directly with guests about the "reality" on the hill.

If extreme weather caused a delayed opening or closure of a particular lift, the Mt. Hood team worked to clearly communicate the news as much in advance as possible directly to the guests. Resort-wide guest service training and recovery techniques were developed to identify and reach out to those guests who might not have been informed in advance, the folks whose experience was most at risk of being compromised by the weather. The results were nothing short of astounding. Even on the worst of weather days positive guest feedback poured in. The resort's owner and CEO, Matthew Drake, was thrilled, "Our proactive efforts at dialogue with our guests resulted in a virtual explosion of guest communication that benefited our processes and people every day."

Mt. Hood Meadows' efforts to reach out to their customers and set expectations openly, honestly and with the opportunity for a shared dialogue established an extraordinary number of loyal customer relationships. Some of the statistics from the 2009–2010 season are worth sharing:

- The resort's web interface facilitated more than 4,200 guest email inquiries, questions and comments.
- The Meadows Facebook® Fan Page grew its subscriber base from 800 to 10,460.
- Over 120 blog posts went out, updating guests about resort happenings.
- A "Guestimonial" section on the website filled up with stories of extraordinary service experiences.
- A weekly emailed newsletter attracted 42,000 subscribers, up from 10,000 the previous season.
- Each week, more than 200 scanned pass-holder surveys provided valuable guest insight and feedback.
- The website's "Conditions" page generated an average of 300,000 unique visits from more than 125,000 unique visitors each month.

- *Skihood.com* was visited almost 1.2 million times (up 16.5 percent) by more than 313,000 unique visitors (up 6.5 percent) for a whopping 3.5 million page views (up 60.5 percent).
- The new communication strategy resulted in guests spending more time obtaining information in advance, which meant better-informed guests arrived at the resort with appropriate expectations.

As Matthew Drake put it, "The ultimate goal of the program was to set our customers' expectations appropriately and then hit those expectations 100 percent of the time. In a sense, we were encouraging the customers to be on the *inside* of the organization so they could know exactly what to expect before and during their visit. They became a part of the Mt. Hood Meadows team and, in effect, they helped us create an incredible experience for them." By leveraging every communication avenue available to the company, the Mt. Hood Meadows team invited customers to be a part of the wooing process. And their guests were more than happy to participate.

Ask Valuable Questions

If you're like most people, you've participated in oodles of customer surveys over the years. If you're like me, you've written letters and emails to companies with the hope that your suggestions will help mend an aspect of the company's service that desperately needs mending. But let me ask you this. Did you ever once believe a company would *change* the way it did business because of your survey answers or your amazingly well-written missives? Just once I'd like to get a non-automated, sincere human reply from one of these companies thanking me for my feedback. The truth is, many surveys and customer input mechanisms are designed as defensive measures—to fend off lawsuits or collect positive facts and figures that can be used to reinforce what the company already believes to be true. You remember that error of seeking confirmation? That's not what I mean by "open dialogue." Creating an open dialogue requires that you ask hard questions to which you don't already have the answers.

I'll never forget a "satisfaction" survey I was given in a hotel a while back. There was an entire section devoted to what appeared to be plumbing and cleanliness issues. Questions like, "Did your towels 'appear' clean?" and "Did your bathtub drain properly?" Now, I don't know about you but, when I stay at a hotel, I don't want the towels to *appear* clean. I would like them to *be* clean! And if the hotel management is so unaware of their plumbing situation that they have to ask how my tub is draining, I can't imagine what else is going on behind the scenes! The point is that most of what is asked on typical customer *satisfaction* surveys has nothing to do with what it takes to create *loyalty*. You can avoid these survey mistakes by following a few simple rules:

Think Like A Customer—Approach the survey questions from a customer's perspective. For example, my loyalty is given to a hotel that has quick and effective check-in services, fast and healthy room service, a clean and well appointed workout facility with good hours. As far as I'm concerned, plumbing and clean towels had better be a given or you've got much bigger problems! Ask your customers questions that are specifically related to things you can control and your areas of strength. Start by looking at the different areas of service you provide or the ways they might use your product or service in their daily lives. Look for those elements that impact the "experience" your customer has with your product or service. I'm hoping that you have a quality product so rather than asking 20 questions about the minutia of quality, you can ask experience-specific questions about the speed of service, efficiency, friendliness, ease of access, etc.

Give Them A Range—Use a five-point scale with number one being "poor" or "strongly disagree" and number five representing "excellent" or "strongly agree." This allows your responders to think in degrees rather than absolutes. If you really want to challenge your assumptions, use only a four-point scale, which doesn't allow anyone a "neutral" response option. That neutral response is sometimes too easy for customers to choose if they have a relationship with you and don't want to hurt your feelings.

Let Them Tell You What's Important—Make sure each question on your survey asks for two different ratings; ask "How are we doing?" as well as "How important is this aspect of our service to you?" This helps you avoid a situation where you have lots of great customer input competing for top priority. Remember you are trying to ensure your customer is telling you what generates loyalty rather than simply what is of interest. I once had a client who spent millions re-organizing his entire operation around low *satisfaction* scores for delivery only to find out later that delivery was not one of the things that kept customers coming back to his company. Let your customers tell you what's important to them so you can focus your resources and energy on those things that generate loyalty.

Keep It Productive (for your customers and yourself)— Don't ask everything under the sun. Remember, you can always do another survey. To get the best response, make sure your questions are specific and actionable and your survey is quick and easy to fill out. Once you have what you believe is your final version go through each question and ask yourself, "What might I do differently in my business based on the answers to this question?" Be sure you make it easy for customers by providing lists of options to choose from as well as spaces in which they can offer detail on open-ended questions. If you are doing an online survey, use drop-down menus with lists of possible answers *and* include boxes in which they can elaborate or provide a response you may not have considered. This creates a quick and easy survey for your customers while allowing you to gather the information in a format that is easy to compile and analyze. If you can't come up with a list of possible responses, take the question off the survey.

Stick With Actionable Items—Ask only about the things you can control and act on. There is nothing worse than being asked to spend time answering a survey about things over which the organization has no control. For example, if you are in a highly regulated industry don't ask how they feel about the regulations you are required to follow. Instead, ask how you can better communicate with them to help them navigate the regulatory changes as they occur. If you own a golf course, don't ask them about the weather. If you own a ski area, don't ask them about the snow conditions. Ask them about specific elements of the overall experience with you as well as how you might be able to better serve them when things that are not in your control conspire to have a negative impact on the customer experience. E.g., "When it's raining what could we do to keep you from going home?"

Referrals Prove Loyalty—Created by one of the fathers of the loyalty movement, Frederick Reichheld, one of the best gauges of a customer's true loyalty to a product or service is called the "Net Promoter® Score" (NPS). This question focuses on where the rubber meets the road when it comes to loyalty. It asks how likely customers are to recommend your product or service to a friend or family member. For this question, you should use a traditional 10-point scale to see just how likely your customers are to "promote" you to others. (See Figure 1, page 74.) Of course, in an ideal world, an NPS of 100 would be great. But, realistically, you need an NPS between 60 and 80 to effectively drive profitability.

How likely are you to recommend to a colleague or friend?

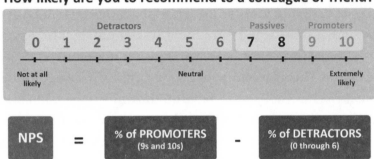

Figure 1. *The Ultimate Question,* Frederick Reichheld

Ask For Suggestions—Make sure you include some global questions that allow customers to work in partnership with you to attract more customers like them. For example, you could ask, "What could we do for you today that would keep you coming back to us year after year/ purchase after purchase?" Hint: You may want to provide a drop-down menu of ideas to cut down on unhelpful responses like, "Give me your product for free!"

Dig For Demographics (for business-to-consumer companies)—Although survey responders can be reticent to provide you with age, education level, income range, etc., these demographic indicators can help you identify the customers that are right for you ... those who are most likely to become profitable and loyal customers. With a sincere assurance that the information will be kept private and not used elsewhere, many survey responders will be happy to help.

Keep It Confidential—When you are initiating an open dialogue with your customer through these methods, you may have to convince your survey participants that you are sincere in your efforts to simply gather data and not use it to annoy or pressure them in any way. Again, when laying the foundation for an ongoing dialogue, you are seeking to build a platform of trust and two-way communication that will move beyond formal surveys at some point in the future. Until that time, you need to make the survey "anonymous" and confidential. Using a vendor like *Survey Monkey*® makes this process easy, as individuals participate via an online, third-party interface that doesn't require them to divulge their identity or personal details unless they wish to provide such information. At the end of each survey, you always want to ask if they would like to be contacted about any issues they have with your organization. This allows them to "opt in" to further discussion with you in a nonthreatening way.

Test The Survey—Before you make the survey available to customers, have some friends test it to make sure the questions are appropriate and easy to understand. Also, when the responses begin to come in, sit down with your team and triple check that the information coming back is actionable. Ask yourselves if the answers supplied are easy to interpret, help you take direct action to increase loyalty with your customers and can be applied to those things within your control.

Take Meaningful Action

Once you have reached out to your customers and they have responded with their input your very next move—even before you look at the data—should be to thank them. Thank them for their time, their effort and their commitment to your success. Now, let me be clear. I'm not talking about an automated response that sends a cold, lifeless, generic thank you message. Any input from your customers or prospects—positive or negative—represents a gift from them. They have shared a little bit of themselves with you. Your immediate response must be to share a little of yourself with them in return. To reach out in a personally relevant way that deepens their trust in you and begins to create a connection between the customer and your company. Anything less is an insult.

Zappos

Here's the response you get if you write a (positive or negative) product review for *Zappos*®...

Thanks for writing a review at *Zappos.com!* Here's the deal:

1. Sometimes it takes 24 hours for a new review to show up.
2. You should have your own blog. You have important things to say.
3. Thanks again for writing a review! Seriously, it's worth repeating.
4. Thanks for writing a review!
5. You rock!

That's just for writing a quick product review. If your customers have gone to the trouble of completing a whole survey, consider acknowledging their efforts with something significant and tangible such as a personal thank you letter with a live signature from the CEO, a certificate for one of your products or services, or even a small donation in their name to a charity. Once you have collected the data, thanked those who provided it and analyzed the results your next step is to keep the conversation going. Regardless of whether the survey results are positive or negative, you have a duty to get back to the customers with an action plan for how you will handle the information. Most of us are quick to act on negative information we receive from our customers. Remember, a true dialogue is created when meaningful actions are taken that address both the bad news and the good news. Here's a great example of a meaningful response from a casino hotel in Las Vegas, Nevada.

The Bellagio

A couple of years ago I traveled to Las Vegas to give a presentation. After the event, I had some time to kill so I decided to try my luck at the roulette wheel, mainly because I couldn't find a lighter to set my money on fire! I was staying at *The Bellagio*, which was owned by Steve Wynn at the time. It was a busy night so the table had quite a few people at it. Most of us had sat through a couple of dealer turns when a woman named Rose took over the dealer position. As soon as she spun the first ball around the wheel, we knew it was a different ballgame. Rose radiated warmth and good humor. She proceeded to find out where all of us were from, laughed and cheered when we won and was clearly remorseful when we lost. We had all begun the night as strangers but, by the time Rose finished her first turn with us, we felt like friends. We all had so much fun with Rose that, when she rotated off of our table, we rotated with her—en masse! Rose and our group of six spent most of the evening together and I'm fairly sure that not a single one of us ended up with more money than we had when we first sat down. As a matter of fact, I lost a bundle! But I think everyone who was with us that evening would agree it was the most fun they had ever had losing money.

I was so impressed with Rose and her ability to make me laugh while I lost money that I wrote Steve Wynn a letter when I got home from that trip. I explained how much fun I had had with Rose and what an amazing asset she was to his organization. I sent the letter off and immediately forgot about it. About two weeks later, I was shocked to find a response in my mailbox from Mr. Wynn himself. In his response he confirmed that he had received and appreciated my letter and he shared with me what *The Bellagio* had done with my input. As a result of my feedback Rose had received a dinner gift certificate to *The Bellagio's* five-star restaurant for herself and her husband. She had also received their "Employee of the Month" award and my letter had been shared at their staff meeting. Along with his kind response Mr. Wynn enclosed a certificate for me, good for one free night at *The Bellagio* during my next trip to Las Vegas. He's no idiot ... he knows I'll probably lose my shirt again! Regardless, I got a meaningful response for sending in a *positive* comment! It's because of actions like this that Steve Wynn has been successful in creating some of the best service experiences in the world. He engaged in a dialogue with me that caused me to care about the success of his business. I came out of this experience knowing how committed he was to me because he showed how much he values his customers and the employees who make his products sing.

Before you read the next section, take a moment to ask yourself what meaningful actions you might be able to take with the information you gain from your customers. Are you communicating back to your customers when they provide you positive feedback as well as negative? Are you sharing a little bit about your values and your strengths when you do it? Are you making it easy for your customers to be open and honest with you by being open and honest with them?

Loyalty Is A Two-Way Street

It follows that if customers are loyal to your company then you should reward them for their behavior. This "carrot" approach to purchasing has been around for a millennium but really started in a tangible way in the 1930s when *S&H Green Stamps*® created the first formalized process for rewarding their clients for repeat purchases. The practice caught on and evolved over time to the first modern-era program started in 1981 by *American Airlines*, who rewarded customers with perks based on the number of miles they had flown.

Frankly, I think calling these programs *loyalty* programs is a bit misleading. They do create repeat purchases but they create them for many reasons that have nothing to do with loyalty. Surely, you have a couple of these program cards in your wallet; travel cards proliferate from *Marriott®* to *Delta®* and *Hertz®* to *Holiday Inn®*. The premise of these programs is simple: if you prove your "loyalty" to us by spending more and more money, we'll give you special treatment that isn't available to "non-loyal" customers. Unfortunately many of the "perks" that are reserved for high-dollar customers are actually basic customer service courtesies that should be available to all customers. In essence, these programs simply offer to make your experience with the company *less painful* if you remain loyal. This has the effect of tethering you to the company out of fear, rather than respect. That's not loyalty. The very programs that should be of benefit to you as a customer backfire and create *more* dissatisfaction than would have existed without any program at all.

In my view, if you have sincerely committed to a path of wooing your customers, you don't need a "loyalty" program to keep them coming back. Think for a minute about the product or service providers to whom you are most loyal. Would earning points make you more loyal to them than you already are? As I think of the companies to which I have given my loyalty, only one of my top 10 has a "loyalty program" and it has nothing to do with whether I come back or not. Their consistent commitment to making my experience with them enjoyable each and every time is what keeps me hooked.

Having stepped off of my soapbox about loyalty programs, I will say that if used only for good and not evil reward programs can be a nice way to thank your customers for giving you the opportunity to serve them again. If you want to create a customer reward or appreciation program, here are some thoughts to keep in mind:

- *Customization Is Essential*: The appreciation shown must be of value to the customers and help them further connect to your brand. This means you have to spend time getting to know your customers and what they value. If you offer me a toaster oven—and I don't want, need or care about a toaster oven—you are just annoying me, not rewarding me.

- *Keep It Realistic*: If you set the bar too high or create barriers that make winning unrealistic for all but a precious few you are more likely to create customer apathy or even antipathy toward the program, which could result in a negative change in their attitudes or buying behaviors.

- *Don't Be Selfish*: If you are truly creating a program that purports to show your appreciation for customers, make sure you are demonstrating your loyalty to them in the process. When you show that you are committed to making them more successful as individuals, you plant the seeds of goodwill that inspire them to do the same for your business.

United Breaks Your Spirit

The best example I have of the lack of a two-way commitment when it comes to such loyalty programs is with the *United Mileage Plus® Program*. As a speaking consultant, I am on the road frequently and I spend a great deal of time in the air. At this point I have achieved a respectable status with most all of the airlines in America but the one I have the highest number of points with is *United Airlines*, which has three levels of loyalty. I have maintained the second level, Premier Executive, for fourteen years running. This status allows me perks while I am traveling like "free" upgrades to First Class and premier seating when there is availability, which gives my six-foot frame three whole inches of extra legroom. It also enables me to get exit row seating and check up to two bags without additional fees. To have access to these minimal perks I must fly 50,000 paid miles (or 60 qualifying segments) per year with the airline. I've been flying so long and so far with *United Airlines* that I am a mere 45,000 miles away from their coveted *Million Miles and Beyond Reward*, which secures its lucky recipients with Premier Executive status for life. This lifetime perk will actually cost the airline nothing extra, while flying to the million mile mark will have cost me well over $400,000 over the course of 20 years.

Here's the thing. Like many others, my business took a hit during the economic recession and thus my travel frequency declined a bit from normal levels. Clearly the airlines also had some difficult times, which is why I assumed they would be interested in ensuring they were keeping their loyal customers loyal. But every day brings a new surprise with our friends at *United*. (Oh, right, like you've never complained about an airline?) At the end of 2009, I knew I was going to be a couple flights short of the 50,000 miles that it would normally take to achieve my coveted Premier

Executive status. After 14 years at that level I thought I had a pretty solid relationship with the airline. Silly me, I imagined that they might take this opportunity to fudge the numbers a little bit and extend my Premier Executive status for another year. I had given so much of myself to *United* for so little in return. Honestly, I had myself convinced that *United* might even send a simple note thanking me for my 950,000 lifetime miles, acknowledging how much they appreciated the miles I did fly in 2009 and extending my Premier Executive status as a thank you for my continued loyalty. After all, even smaller hotel programs were doing this left and right. Instead, I received a computer-generated basic-level card in the mail.

Not one to let sleeping dogs lie, I set about trying to contact someone at the airline who might be able to acknowledge my loyalty and extend my status. After multiple failed attempts, I finally tracked down the direct email address for the President of *United Airlines* and was immediately put into the executive response queue. After six phone calls and three emails, I was finally told that I would not be granted the mere 2,000 miles I needed to retain my status. However, *United Airlines* would graciously *allow me* to *purchase* the miles I needed for the not-so-small fee of $1,000. That's right, folks. I could spend *another* $1,000 to reward myself.

There were so many things wrong with *United's* call on this I could do an entire chapter on it but here's the bottom line. Don't let your *loyalty* program become something that hurts you rather than helps you. Done poorly, this will not only irreparably damage your business, but it has the potential to create a *Serial Killer* customer. Just ask *United Airlines.*

Vanitylab

On the other hand Angie Hofelich, owner of *Vanitylab Salon, Spa & Shop (www.vanitylab.com)* in Westlake, Ohio, has found a way to honor her loyal customers in a way that is truly wooing not only these customers but also future customers as well. Angie gives special gifts to her top 200 clients on top of the usual discounts they receive. "One time, we got a special lot of OPI° nail polish. So we thanked our top clients for their business with a fun invitation for a free polish." Another time, they sent their top 50 clients invites for a complimentary tan at a nearby spray-tanning salon. "Recently, we've begun to ask some of our top clients to help us 'model' our new services. It's really a win-win situation. They get complimentary services and we get the opportunity to introduce them to something they will hopefully love." Angie and her team have even found a way to thank extra special clients and build their business at the same time. "To thank our top client for her business, we hosted a spa party for her and three of her friends. We had a blast and so did she. Now her friends are customers too!" Now that's a loyalty program I can get behind!

Turn The Dialogue Into A Partnership

In Rule 2 we talked about how social networking and the power of one can affect your business. Here are some terrific examples that demonstrate how you can use the social web to promote positive growth for your business. The popularity of the social web now allows you to create new levels of dialogue with your customers. Some entrepreneurs have even created entire business models around customer partnerships that fuel their bottom lines. For example, Jake Nickell and Jacob Dehart were just out of high school when they created what is now a successful T-shirt company called *Threadless* *(www.threadless.com)* with annual sales of $30 million and as many as 700,000 customers.[7] How did these guys do it? Customers of *Threadless* not only get to buy the company's cutting edge T-shirts, they also get to design them. Here's how it works. Every week, customers upload their T-shirt design suggestions to the site. About 800 or so erstwhile designers compete to be among the six that get to see their creations printed. Visitors to the site score designs on a scale of zero to five and the *Threadless* staff selects the winners from the most popular entrants. The six lucky artists each get $2,000 in cash and merchandise and the company gets a battle-tested design. *Threadless* sells out of every T-shirt they produce.

This model works because *Threadless* has created a website that is a growth traffic machine. The theory is exactly like the old *Fabergé Organic Shampoo* commercial in which everyone tells two friends and so on. A simple dialogue between *Threadless* and its customers ensures that their site visitors will continue to grow exponentially. Designers invite friends online to vote for their designs. Those friends often then submit their own designs. Designers earn purchase credits by inviting friends.

And wearers photographed modeling T-shirts earn even more credits. It's dialogue on top of dialogue, all driving dollars to *Threadless's* bottom line. I'm not suggesting every company can create a model that is based solely on customer partnerships but to woo your customer for the long term, this kind of ongoing involvement is essential.

Some organizations have become so good at wooing customers into partnership with them that they are teaching other companies how to do it. *Zappos (www.zappos.com),* the $1.2 billion e-commerce juggernaut, has created a philosophy and a model of execution that makes good on CEO Tony Hsieh's promise to be a "service company that happens to sell shoes, clothing, eyewear, handbags and a bunch of other stuff." Hsieh is widely regarded as one of the most innovative marketers of all time.[8] Bestselling author and marketing guru Seth Godin has likened Hsieh's ability to use technology to create enduring customer connections to the Beatles' ability to animate their teenage fans. Wow.

Zappos has opened up its entire operation to customers. This allows customers to feel like they are a part of the process and encourages them to communicate regularly with the organization to ensure *Zappos* is getting better and better every day. Here are just a few of the things *Zappos* does to create this high level of involvement and ongoing dialogue:

- *Easy Access*—Web visitors have 24/7 access to customer assistance via an 800 number that appears on every web page.

- *Free Shipping*—All orders include free shipping (both ways) and a magnificent 365-day return policy.
- *Interaction*—There are no call-time or sales-based performance measures for call center staff; they want their employees to talk to customers.
- *Quit Pay*—*Zappos* pays employees $2,000 to quit if, after five weeks of culture, core values, customer service and warehouse training they don't think they will like working for the company.
- *Sharing*—*Zappos* shares its core values on its shipping boxes to encourage customers to tell them how they have achieved or haven't achieved their goals.
- *Free Tours*—*Zappos* hosts a free tour of its headquarters every couple of hours so customers and competitors alike can see how they do it. Just call the company when you're in town (Henderson, Nevada) and someone will pick you up in the *Zappos* shuttle.
- *Tweets*—Tony Hsieh has over 1.7 million followers on *Twitter* and posts regularly with interesting insights.

Could it be true? Just ask Tara Hunt, a San Francisco marketing executive for *Intuit*®, who posted to her *Twitter* followers when she was having a shipping issue with *UPS*®. To her surprise, she got a response from Tony Hsieh, who had started following her tweets after he met her at a meeting a year earlier. He was having dinner with the Western Region President for *UPS* and sent Tara a message saying she should expect a call. Within five minutes her phone rang. The next morning at 9:00 a.m. her package was delivered, along with a bouquet of flowers and a box of chocolates.[9]

Luxor Executive Car Service

One company with which I have the greatest level of loyalty is the car service I use to get me to the airports for my 50 or so trips a year. *Luxor Executive Car Service (www.luxorexecutivecar.com)* was a small offshoot of the local cab company that two brothers turned into a personalized service with an almost rabid customer following. How did they do it? Through an "ease of service" and communication that has customers helping *them* provide great service at every turn!

My schedule tends to be somewhat fluid and requires constant juggling. So, for years, I hesitated to use a car service. Despite the fact that it added at least 30 minutes to each end of my trips, I drove myself to the airport and parked in long-term parking. With my departure time completely under my control I never feared arriving at the airport late because of a tardy taxi. I lamented the extra time (which over the number of trips I take a year really added up) but didn't think there was an alternative I could count on. Until one day when I was preparing to take friends from out of town to the airport for their flight home and I discovered I had a flat tire! After a frantic few moments and some phone calls to local taxi and car services, I happened upon *Luxor*. The first thing that was different from my other calls was the live person who answered the phone. "This is Jonathan, how may I help you?" I quickly shared my desperate need to get someone to take my friends to the airport. Jonathan matched my tone of urgency and said, "I think we can help. Can you hold the line for a minute while I make a call?"

Well, lo and behold, even though all of *Luxor's* cars were in service, Jonathan was able to call another service that they used for back up and had a car to my house in a remarkable 15 minutes, whisking my friends off to their flight. Shortly after the car arrived, Jonathan called me back to make sure all was well. I was so astonished by this level of service that I decided to throw caution to the wind and try *Luxor* for myself.

After six years, and I can't tell you how many trips, not once has *Luxor* arrived at my house less than 10 minutes *early*. What's more, their drivers (almost all of whom I now know well) are constantly updating me on relevant changes *inside* the airport that they have heard about from other customers. The partnership I have with *Luxor* is multi-faceted and gains strength at every level. As you read the following points, consider how your business might do something similar to build loyalty with your customers:

- *Luxor Instills Confidence*—I know beyond a shadow of a doubt that *Luxor* does what they say they will do. They deliver on the basics of their business with 100 percent quality. Whenever I call, I know that I will be treated with efficiency and courtesy. Most importantly, I know that no matter how inefficient *my* travel process is (I've been known to forget I was traveling until two hours before I needed a car) they will be there, on time with a clean car and a smiling driver, ready to whisk me to my destination.

- *Luxor Empowers Me*—Each time I call for a pick-up, Jonathan or Max (his brother) asks what airline I am flying and relays that information to the driver. The driver then knows to mention any changes he has heard about through the grapevine that might affect my travel. "*United* changed it's configuration at TSA," he might say, "So you'll want to go through the far end because no one seems to know about that line yet." Little nuggets of information like this save me time and energy once I am in the airport. In return, I share information that I have after my trips so they can pass it on to their other clients. This give and take not only builds my relationship with them but also creates the feeling they care about my entire travel experience ... not just their portion of it.

- *Luxor Shares My Pain*—During the downturn in 2009, it made sense that many of *Luxor's* clients probably began using them less frequently as both business and leisure travel were severely impacted. Many companies took that opportunity to *increase* their costs to "maintain their profitability," showing a complete disregard for their customers. *Luxor* not only didn't increase their rates but also called their customers to let us know that they felt our pain. During calls to their best customers, they offered a rate *reduction* and expressed sincere hope we would all be here when the economy came back. I know, as an entrepreneur myself how painful that rate decrease must have been for *Luxor* but they did it because it was the right thing to do *and* because I think they really do care about helping their customers.

Similar to advocacy, this level of loyalty is stronger and deeper. It means that *both* company and customer care about each other's success and take actions to help one another, even when doing so is a hardship. I recommended *Luxor* to everyone I knew before 2009 but how many times do you think I have told that rate decrease story to people since then? What do you think my reaction will be when *Luxor's* rates go back up, which they inevitably will? Even if they go up higher than they were before the decrease, will I leave? Never. *Luxor* has demonstrated that they are more interested in me than in my money; they are in partnership with me and I would not think of letting them down by going elsewhere. How many of your customers could say that about you?

How Well Does Your Dialogue Woo?

- What businesses do I frequent even though they are more expensive or further away, etc? Why do I stay with them? Is there anything that could be adapted to my business? What businesses do I recommend to my friends and why?

- Do I have processes in place to gather customer information and build a useable database? If no, what do I need to do to start? If yes, how can I expand upon the information I have? If I do have the information, am I sharing it with my entire team and proactively utilizing the data to improve service?

- Am I talking openly with my *Steady Eddies* on a regular basis? Am I finding out what else I can do to help them move to advocacy? Am I giving them as much as I'm asking them to give me?

- What processes do I have in place that make customers want to keep coming back? Am I using those processes consistently and rewarding loyalty with ease of use, ease of interaction, ease of repeat purchase?

- What things do I do before, during and after customer transactions that might make someone think twice about switching to another provider?

- Am I helping my *Diehard Advocates* spread the word? If no, what can I do to encourage and enable them to recruit new customers for me? What could I give them in return for their efforts on my behalf?

RULE 5

* * *

Set The Bar And Meet It

"Quality in a product or service is not what you put into it. It is what the client or customer gets out of it."
— *Peter Drucker*

"Letting your customers set your standards is a dangerous game, because the race to the bottom is pretty easy to win. Setting your own standards—and living up to them— is a better way to profit. Not to mention a better way to make your day worth all the effort you put into it."
— *Seth Godin*

When I began in the consumer database business almost 20 years ago, we had a hard time convincing companies that it made sense for them to even collect information about their customers much less use it to create a deeper relationship. The pendulum swung all the way back in the late 1990s and early 2000s when all we heard about was "exceeding customer expectations" and creating "exquisite service experiences." Many business owners are still pursuing these absurd goals today. I certainly hope you're not one of them.

Don't get me wrong. If you're running a five-star, five-diamond, multimillion-dollar resort and charging clients exorbitant fees you darn well better be providing excessively exceptional service. Because that is exactly the expectation you have chosen to set with your customers. What is important to understand is that you have a choice as to *where* you set the expectation bar for your customers. Once you've made that decision you have no choice but to meet those expectations every time. Shoot too low and you disappoint them. Shoot too high and you confuse them. That's what I mean when I say that "exceeding expectations" is an absurd goal.

Put your customer hat on.

- *What businesses set clear expectations for you and meet them consistently?*
- *Do you feel loyal to them?*
- *What businesses over-promise and under-deliver?*
- *When they do, do you go back?*
- *Has a company ever gone overboard and turned you off?*

Aim For Consistency And Predictability

So what expectations have you set for your customers and clients? If you're like most entrepreneurs, you started your company aiming to do "your very best" ... but what does that really mean? And how will your customers know how to judge you if you don't give them some criteria for measurement? Take a minute right now to review your current advertising, website, email campaigns, retail space, community involvement, sales pitches and packages from your customers' point of view. Look at all the external messages that create first impressions about your business. What do they tell you about where you have set your bar?

Entrepreneurs like to think and dream big. So it may come as no surprise that a lot of companies run into trouble when they fail to align their customers' expectations with what they can really deliver. When you're imagining all of the possibilities for your business it's easy to make promises that you're not yet sure you can keep. Imagine if *Federal Express* didn't have the processes in place behind the scenes to make good on their promise to deliver, "when it absolutely positively has to be there." Imagine if they'd made that promise and then only gotten it there *most* of the time.

Think about the wording in your external messages that describe expectations they set for your customers. Now, shift back into business owner mode and make a list of the "deliverables" that your company is capable of providing consistently and with a high level of quality.

Do the two lists match up? Many businesses struggle because they set unrealistic expectations that they can't meet consistently. This disappoints their customers and injures the trust between parties before the relationship has even begun. Where this disappointment occurs most frequently is in the handoff between the sales personnel— "Of course we can ship that to you by tomorrow and in purple!"—and the service provider who is saddled with ... well, you know ... reality!

The truth of the matter is that your customers *want* you to set expectations, the kind of expectations they can take to the bank. They want you to commit to doing something and then do it. Every. Single. Time. That's what builds trust and loyalty. You don't need to exceed expectations at all! You just need to be clear about what your strengths are, tell customers what they can expect from you and then make sure you live up to those expectations. Remember, where you set the bar is the promise you make to your customers.

Unlike the proverbial horseshoes and grenades comparison, setting the bar for your company requires precision. And conversation. Deciding on a service expectation should involve everyone on your team and create some robust arguments. If you are doing it right. Customer expectations shouldn't be "stretch" goals that you hope to achieve either. This is not your mission or a vision for your future. Customer expectations need to represent those things you can, beyond a shadow of a doubt, knock out of the ballpark every time. The beautiful thing is that it doesn't matter *where* you set the bar. Just make sure you deliver on your promise consistently.

Ryan Air

One of my all-time favorite customer expectation-setting stories is *Ryan Air*, the Irish airline that has set a standard for *low service*, which gained them the loyalty of literally millions of flyers. How the heck do you do that you ask? Well, *Ryan Air* decided they were going to be the low-cost, truly no-frills airline. They wanted to be the airline of choice for people who were interested in a great deal and *nothing* else. So they designed their entire business model around *not* serving customers. Their planes don't have seat pockets (emergency cards are stuck to the seat in front of you). If you want service, you have to pay extra—including printed boarding passes (€40), checking bags and more. There are notices on the overhead bins informing you that, if you want anything to drink or eat, you had better be ready to pay. In their advertising they even reinforce their low expectations model by announcing plans to charge customers for in-flight restroom use and offer "standing room only" tickets for those who want an even better deal. (Neither of these programs was implemented for obvious reasons.)

Ryan Air set the bar low, told customers exactly what to expect and then consistently met those low expectations. Ironically, meeting their intentionally low expectations has allowed them to create an incredibly efficient airline that boasts the best on-time stats in the European market and ranks as the number one airline in Europe for international passengers. Now this example might seem antithetical to the idea of wooing your customers. But it is in fact a perfect example of how one entrepreneur took a great strength (cost efficiency), built a business model around that strength, made sure customers were crystal clear in their expectations, and met those expectations every time. Because of their clarity and consistency, *Ryan Air* wooed literally millions of customers to their doors.

As an entrepreneur, it's easy to get overly enthusiastic about serving your customers. Hey, you're giving it your all, right? But your enthusiasm could actually be scaring away some potential buyers. "Oh, I don't need all that. I just need a simple widget." Moreover, putting on a show of exceeding expectations for your customers can leave you stressed and burned out in no time at all. If you are rolling out the red carpet as a default mechanism consider the fact that you may be avoiding doing the work of matching your unique strengths with your customers' needs.

Emmy's Spaghetti Shack

Here's a trick. This restaurant used low expectations to set high expectations for just a few key areas of their business. I live in San Francisco so everything is either up or down a hill. Thankfully, downhill from my home, there is a small, hole-in-the-wall restaurant called *Emmy's Spaghetti Shack*. It sits on a bit of an "iffy" corner near a *Pizza Hut*® and two bars. When I first moved to the neighborhood I noticed that each evening, when I drove by *Emmy's* on my way home from work, there was invariably a line of people waiting to get in. Now this place has an unpolished exterior, bars on the windows, pretty much all the signs of a rough establishment. But when I took a closer look at the crowd standing in line I realized they ran the gamut from 20-something hipsters to 60-something suburbanites. Eventually, my curiosity got the better of me and I decided to check it out. When I inquired at the counter, I was told that this 10-table restaurant had an hour long wait ... an *hour*? They had tattered red vinyl booths for Pete's sake! These booths looked as though they hadn't been really cleaned since they were swiped out of a diner in the 1960s. An *hour*?

Wrestling with a mix of frustration (hunger), disbelief and simple curiosity, I waited. During my wait, the well tattooed, six-foot-tall, Harley-jacketed host couldn't have been nicer. And two servers did a great job of making sure those of us waiting outside (in the now drizzling weather) had a chance to order something warm to drink while we waited. Nonetheless, I started to ask my future potential fellow diners a few questions, "Why are we all waiting in the rain? Is this place really worth it? Have you ever eaten here before?" The responses I got wowed me ...

"The Truffled Filet Mignon is to die for"

"The Lemon Chilean Sea Bass can't be beat."

"Best Meatballs I have ever had."

What the heck was going on? This place looked like it should be attached to a gas station and selling reheated burritos. Once I finally got my coveted table my experience couldn't have been more satisfying.

The painfully young wait-staff were not only incredibly nice and wonderfully efficient but they were also knowledgeable about the dishes, how they were prepared, and had useful opinions about what we might like based on our preferences. The food ... well suffice it to say that *Emmy's* has become a weekly event for me and my family thanks to the ever changing menu and the innovative skills of the chef. And every single time we go in, and the Harley-jacketed host greets us like family, we know we're going to enjoy the same great experience.

Emmy's didn't want me to have high expectations for the building, the seating or table accessibility. Those weren't their strengths. Their strengths were marvelous gourmet food and friendly, unpretentious service. *Emmy's* decided they wanted to be a great neighborhood restaurant that also happened to be a great experience, without all the fluff. They've succeeded in spades!

Virgin America

The best example I have found for setting high expectations and meeting them is in an industry cited most frequently as one of the worst for their treatment of customers ... the airline industry. For those of you who haven't tried them yet, run ... don't walk to your nearest *Virgin America* flight. Other airlines *say* they care about their customers, but in my opinion, only *Virgin America* makes good on that promise.

Your experience begins at the check-in counter where you are greeted with eye contact, a smile and what appears to be a sincere interest in you and your travel plans. Now, I know what you're saying … I said it too … this must be an anomaly … I got the one nice counter person … surely they can't have more people like this! To my surprise, the positive and downright entertaining experience continued from the ticket counter to the actual gate. (Don't get me started on security … that's a whole other book!) At the gate, I began to get a bit suspicious. Again, I was greeted with a cheerful demeanor along with a discussion of autumn in New York, which was my final destination. As the journey continued, bizarre things occurred. A flight attendant put my bag in the overhead compartment for me (gasp!). Another flight attendant held a jovial conversation with a customer about the cool lighting in the cabin (purple). I was presented with the opportunity to order from a full range of drinks and snacks without having to wait for a flight attendant to come by that one time per flight to provide me with my cup of water. In no time at all my selections were efficiently delivered to me by yet another agreeable flying partner (what? another one?). No one banged my elbows with a cart. No one snickered at passengers from the back galley. I didn't feel alone in a crowd. In fact, I began to feel like I never wanted to leave! As we touched down I actually said to my seatmate, "I *so* wish this flight had been a bit *longer*!" What? Have I gone mad?

Now with all this raving, I know you're probably saying, "Oh, sure! They must have a million-dollar training budget along with perks galore to get such great service out of their staff." So you'll be glad to know that I did some research. I found that not only does *Virgin America* have a *smaller* training budget per employee than any of their larger competitors *(Delta, United, American)* but they also are right on par with the industry standard in terms of salaries and benefits. So what is their secret? What *Virgin America* is doing differently costs them absolutely nothing and is easy to execute, especially for companies that have hundreds of employees rather than thousands. In every step of *Virgin America's* employee process—from hiring, to training, to reviews to leadership communication— the airline is focused on one thing: a common sense of purpose around "making flying fun again." The things they do exceedingly well cost them nothing ... a smile, eye contact at every step in the process and a laser-focus on remembering that it is because of every customer's decision to fly with them, that they are able to continue putting fun back in the skies. What I learned from *Virgin America* is that the most important things to a customer tend to be the things that cost us nothing to provide ... attitude, a smile, sincerity, a common sense of purpose and a little bit of fun. See you on my next flight!

Start The Way You Wish To Continue

If you are truly committed to winning customers over for the long term you need to start the conversation and then be diligent about keeping it going. I'm sure your customers get a ton of love during the initial selling process. But are you cherishing the relationship you have with them on an ongoing basis? It seems most organizations spend an inordinate amount of time, money and energy getting customers in the door and then very little making sure they continue to get great service once the honeymoon is over. A little story that I heard somewhere years ago demonstrates this point better than I ever could. It goes a something like this ...

A man dies and finds himself at the pearly gates. The guard at the gates is holding a clipboard checking in people as they arrive. The guard looks up and smiles as he sees the new gentleman in line. He says, "You are so lucky that you died today! There's a special we're offering today only!"

"Really?" says the man.

"Yeah, you get to choose whether you want to go to Heaven or Hell."

The man asks, "How will I know which to choose?"

The guard quickly responds, "Not to worry! We let you stay a day in each place so you can make an informed decision about where you want to spend all eternity."

The man says, "Okay. I think I'd like to go to Hell first."

The guard smiles and motions him into an elevator directly behind him. "Great! Down you go!"

The doors open up onto a white sandy beach. People are playing in the surf, drinking drinks with little umbrellas, and dancing to a Calypso band. It's absolutely ... well, Heaven! The man spends an enjoyable day, comes back up, steps out of the elevator and says, "That was wonderful! I can't wait to see what Heaven is like!"

Back into the elevator and up he goes! The doors open on white fluffy clouds, harp music and lots of smiling, happy people. It's very nice but not really very exciting. After his day, the man goes back down in the elevator and says to the guard, "I can't believe I am going to say this but ... I'd like to go to Hell please." The guard says no problem and down the man goes.

This time when the doors open, instead of seeing the beach and Calypso band he's greeted by people running, screaming, fire, and brimstone. He stands there ... dumbfounded. The Devil comes up to him and barks, "What's your problem? Get in here!" And the man responds, stuttering, "There must be some mistake! I was here yesterday! There was a beach and drinks with little umbrellas! What happened?!"

The Devil responds, "We get this all the time. Yesterday you were a prospect. Today you're a customer!"

Of course, no one would ever do this intentionally. But it happens all the time. So take a minute right now to think about your initial sales pitch. Okay, now think about the reality of working with your business. Do the two match up? How often are you your own worst enemy when it comes to following through on the promises you make? As a business owner, you may be intimately involved in the initial selling process, particularly with larger clients. But, once signed, do you place those clients in the care of others who (you hope) will follow through on your promises? How well do you communicate your promises to the team that's responsible for fulfilling them?

Become A Recovery Expert

No matter how hard you try, no matter how great your processes, there will be times when you fail your customers. Some of the failures will be small, like delivering the wrong meal or a typo in a marketing piece before it goes to print. Others will be so big you won't be able to imagine how your customer will ever forgive you. Everything from life and death situations in the world of hospitals and doctors to multi-million dollar recalls. Thankfully, in the world of business, forgiveness is truly divine. It turns out that, just as with personal relationships, the more you and your customer go through together successfully the deeper the bond between you. In fact, research has demonstrated that when companies fail a customer, and then recover well, that customer is likely to increase his or her feelings of loyalty by as much as 40 percent.[10]

Now I'm not suggesting that failure is something to be embarked upon with glee. Rather, I am suggesting that you need to acknowledge that mistakes sometimes happen and be prepared with an airtight strategy for recovery that will enable you and your team to take advantage of this customer service phenomenon. Certainly, there are some customers who will never get over a failure but most will be willing to forgive if you approach them the right way. Here are a few things worth considering in the development of your recovery process...

1. *What Kinds of Issues Are There?*—There are two distinct types of customer service issues: those caused by you and those caused by the customer. Research shows that customers create one-third of their own problems. If you wish to maintain the customer relationship and preserve your company's reputation, however, both types of issues

should be handled gracefully and without regard for who is at fault.

2. *Have You Prepared Your Team?*—Being prepared to handle issues gracefully means you should run scenarios with your teams that identify possible solutions ahead of time. This ensures that your solutions, when needed, will be well thought through and easy to act on. If you have necessary processes or procedures that you know are difficult or confusing for your customers, you should find ways to help your employees prepare for the issues that will arise. Most of the business leaders with whom I have worked know exactly where the "wheels come off the wagon" for their customers. Are you preparing your people with the knowledge and accountability to do what's right to woo that customer back when things go awry?

3. *How Will You Learn About Issues?*—Customer information comes in from all different directions. Sometimes the customer will call you directly. Sometimes a delivery person will overhear an issue. Sometimes a lack of response on the part of a customer will indicate there may be a problem. In other situations, however, one of your *Steady Eddies* might, in an effort to avoid confrontation, simply slip away from you after a dissatisfying experience. To avoid this, you and your employees need to be vigilant about watching for warning signs. If there is any doubt about a particular

customer exchange, you or your employees need to feel comfortable asking the customer if anything is wrong. Remember, the best time and place to correct a problem is when and where it occurs. As we discussed earlier, it's also imperative that you watch the online social networks just in case one of your customers decides to share a concern or gripe with others before talking with you.

4. *How Will Issues Be Communicated?*—Once an issue has been identified, the particulars of that issue need to be communicated clearly and immediately to the person in your organization who can take decisive action to remedy the situation. Having a plan in place for how issues will be communicated is essential. If a housekeeper simply tells the other housekeepers about an issue, you may miss your chance to act. On the other hand, if that housekeeper knows she can take time out to immediately report the problem to the manager on duty, you're in business. Your entire company has to be able to act as one when a problem arises. So it is essential that you have a plan and that you have communicated that plan to your entire staff.

5. *Who Is Empowered To Resolve Them?*—Many entrepreneurs have smaller organizations in which the standing rule is, "Take any issues directly to the owner." As omnipotent as some of us are, this kind of a plan is rarely sufficient. I'm not

suggesting you need a multi-level Gantt chart delineating decision-making responsibilities. But you do need one or two backup decision makers who are empowered to deal directly with issues in the event that you are unavailable. Moreover, those who are acting as your backup must have the knowledge and authority to act as your *surrogate* not just a stopgap until you are available.

6. *Apologies Are Just A Beginning*—An immediate and gracious apology is critical. However, apologizing only works if it's followed by meaningful action. I'm willing to bet you can recall a time when you were told, "I'm so sorry that happened but I'm not able to help. That takes a manager and she's not here right now." They might as well be saying, "Gee, I'm so sorry you have such bad luck, sucker. I'm sure glad I'm not you!" By all means apologize but don't forget to follow through!

7. *Aim For More Than Fairness*—What's the best way to follow through on an apology? What's a fair solution to the problem? The focus of any good recovery shouldn't be on cost (i.e., "What's it going to cost me to make this right?"). Instead, your solution to any customer issue should be based on the value of the relationship to your company. What is this person worth to you? What's his or her lifetime value? And more importantly, what kind of *story* will he or she tell ... and to whom? Put yourself in the customer's shoes. Isn't being

treated with respect and fairness usually more than enough to convince you to give the company a second chance?

> ## Put your customer hat on.
>
> - *What's the best recovery a company has provided for you?*
> - *What did they do to make sure you felt they were doing all they could to help?*
> - *How did you feel about them later?*
> - *Were you more loyal than before?*
> - *Have you ever gotten an apology and then nothing else? How did it feel?*
> - *What more could the business have done to recover from the incident?*

Jessie et Laurent

Jessie Boucher of *Jessie et Laurent*, the gourmet dining service we read about earlier, has a wonderful way of phrasing it. She says she makes a "human promise" to her customers that she will use all of her resources to make sure the company delivers on the customer's expectations and when they don't, she will do her very best to come to a "fair and collaborative" solution. The story she tells is about a meal delivery customer who wasn't at home for her delivery when Jessie's driver, as is the practice, left the prepared food in a cooler at a prearranged spot near her door. Unfortunately, this client had forgotten it was her delivery day and the food, which remained unnoticed for three days, spoiled. Upon her discovery of the cooler, the customer called Jessie and explained the situation. Even though it was the customer's fault, Jessie considered the long-term value of the customer and suggested they split the cost of a new order to be sent out right away so she wouldn't have to wait another week for her regular delivery. Jessie asked the customer if she felt that would be fair and the customer agreed and was grateful. In this case, the customer reached out to Jessie so she could make it right. And Jessie was able to keep and even deepen the relationship further with a simple solution that cost her half the price of one meal, delivered.

Continental Airlines

My dear friend Margaret Heffernan, author of the two wonderful business books, *The Naked Truth* and *How She Does It*, told me a great story a while back about an interaction she had with her airline of choice, *Continental Airlines*. Margaret flies in and out of Gatwick Airport in the United Kingdom and much of her speaking is done in the United States. So you can imagine what kind of frequent flyer status she has with this particular airline. On this occasion, she had just been through, as she says in her lovely British accent, "a rough patch" with *Continental* that included missed flights, misdirected luggage, double seat assignments and myriad other issues. In other words, she had been beaten and bloodied by a company that should have been treating her like royalty. After one final straw, which cost her not only precious time and sanity but also cash, Margaret decided to take pen to paper (or keyboard to computer) and write a letter of complaint. "In my rather long letter," she said, "I tried to be reasonable, rational, specific and fair. I tried to explain, as one business person to another, how their business's failures had impacted me. When I got home, I posted the letter to the most senior executives of the airline, never expecting a response."

Well, not only did *Continental* surprise her with their response by remedying the initial problems but they also went the extra mile by following up months later to ensure the recovery process had worked to her satisfaction. Margaret's story went from one of pain and suffering to a story of ardent advocacy. "I have stopped telling calamitous travel stories. Now I have a different tale to tell because the response I got was astonishing: first an email, then a phone call, then personal face-to-face attention. But here's the thing that truly impressed me. About two months later, the senior executive followed up with an email asking how I felt now that some time had passed *and* he thanked me for having given his company the opportunity 'to redeem themselves'." Closing the loop ensures that your dialogue continues and that your customer knows you care about him or her, not only for the short term but also for the long run.

Ritz Carlton

Not long ago, I stayed at the *Ritz Carlton*® in Westchester, New York the evening before a big presentation. I arrived late but was not spared the usual fabulous guest treatment as I was shown to a beautiful suite overlooking the city. It was well past midnight by the time I had unpacked and settled in for a lovely sleep. I hadn't had the light off for more than five minutes when I heard the unmistakable sound of wildlife rifling through a large potted plant. I wasn't sure what it was exactly but I was darn sure I didn't want it in my room, so I quickly called the front desk to report what I thought was a mouse in my room. The attendant at the front desk apologized profusely and said she would send someone "right up."

I got out of bed, put on my plush robe and then sat down again to keep an eye on the plant for what I imagined would be a long wait while someone from engineering was called to assist me. I couldn't have been more surprised when, less than five minutes later, a discreet knock sounded on my door. I opened it to the manager of the hotel and a bellman. The manager apologized profusely and explained that there was a rather large construction project going on next-door that had dislodged some local field mice who were, naturally, inclined to find new accommodations at the *Ritz*. They had been working on the problem every day and he was extremely distressed that they hadn't been able to resolve the issue before my arrival. The manager and his bellman had come to my room armed with two possible solutions: they could quickly move me to another room or they could take a shot at catching the little guy and moving *him*. As the hour was so late, I opted for the room change. I didn't even need to pack, just set everything on the luggage cart. The bellman had the new key in hand and efficiently moved me three doors down the hall. In less than 10 minutes I was settled into the plush linens in my new, mouse-less room. Now, even if the story ended there it would be an awesome story of recovery but it continued. The next morning, when I checked out, I found that my entire room cost (over $500) had been removed from the bill to make up for the inconvenience. Now *that's* what I call complete recovery!

It was obvious to me that the *Westchester Ritz Carlton* has a well-defined recovery process that includes communicating issues to the manager immediately and arming the manager with recovery actions before he even knocks on a guest's door. He had, after all, arrived with both a bellman and a new room key, which made resolution of my issue at that late hour easy and painless for me. Not only did the hotel have a process in place to ensure that I got a good night's sleep, but they wowed me the next morning by backing up their apologies with real dollars. Do you think I'll ever stay there again? You bet! Every time I get a chance.

I know most of us don't have the deep pockets that the *Ritz Carlton* has for recovery and I'm not suggesting that expensive solutions are always necessary. What's most important is to keep and deepen the relationship with a resolution that feels more than fair to both you and your valued customer. That night, I was already thrilled with how the *Ritz Carlton* dealt with my issue but my story would still have been about a critter in my room. Once they closed the loop by removing the charges for the room, my story became about the amazing recovery. So remember to ask yourself, "What is the story they will tell their friends and family? Will they say you treated them fairly and did all you could?"

Delta Recovery Center

Some of life's moments are just too good not to share. This is one of them. It involves an organization that tried to get ahead of the recovery curve when they foresaw trouble. But their good intentions went awry and I still laugh about it to this day. It happened in an airport in the Midwest as I was walking down the concourse. Down the hallway in the distance, I spotted an enormous sign announcing the "Delta Recovery Center." The average person might have breezed right past but customer service is one of my areas of expertise. My first impression was to chuckle at the word *recovery*. Recovery is an *internal* word that really has nothing to do with customers and essentially announces your company's intention to fail.

My second thought, which garnered a guffaw, was that if *Delta* needs an entire *center* to handle their customer service failures ... what does that say about their processes to begin with? When I finally reached the center itself, I literally stopped dead in my tracks and howled like crazy person. The space was vast. It had been arranged neatly with a red rope maze that contained no fewer than ten switchbacks, all leading to a massive counter with ... wait for it ... *one* customer service representative and one lonely computer terminal! This tale is a good reminder that you should fix systemic issues rather than continue to attempt to recover from a problem that is occurring over and over again. Recovery is not the answer when a change in your processes could preempt the issue in the first place. And for goodness' sake, don't announce your intention to fail with an enormous sign. It's just not good for business.

Measure Your Progress, Tweak Your Process

Once you have committed to broadening your understanding of your customers' needs and creating a fully integrated service strategy, the challenge becomes ensuring that you keep the process moving forward. Not many of us would have excelled in school had there not been some kind of benchmark or grade that was gauging our performance. Most world-class organizations measure their ability to meet their customers' needs via seemingly duplicative methods, all of which are necessary to understand the full profile of their customers. These often include a combination of industry-wide surveys, customized consumer research, analysis of customer transaction patterns and mechanisms that collect front-line, customer feedback. It is through the checks and balances of these methods that organizations are able to discern the true voice of their customer. Below are some important things to remember when determining what metrics to use to accurately and appropriately measure your progress with customers and unearth possible process tweaks.

- *Ask Questions You Can Act On*—Make sure you are asking your customers questions about practices you are actually willing and able to address. Remember, your customers' time—and your time—is limited. So focus on what is important to know, not what is nice to know.

- *Beware Of Self-Defeating Activity*—Make sure the things you are measuring are driving the appropriate behaviors from your employees. Remember that there are many metrics that are easy to track but may have a negative correlation with increased revenue or return visits. Tracking things that appear on the surface to drive your ability to woo customers may in fact drive the opposite. I am always stunned when customer service call centers evaluate their people on the *amount of time* they spend on the phone with customers who call in with an issue or question. Some call centers evaluate their agents on how quickly they can get off the phone rather than measuring how frequently they were able to resolve customers' issues. Years ago I had a client who was positively beaming about their "great service" because the data showed that 90 percent of their calls were less than two minutes long. She stopped beaming when I asked her to check how many times calls were transferred to other agents. We discovered that the average customer was being transferred no fewer than five times before an issue was resolved. The center's measurement was driving the wrong behavior.

- *Let Your Customers Take The Lead*—Instead of trying to be all things to all people, let your customers lead you to the areas you need to focus on to drive their loyalty. Creating a truly customer-focused culture requires you to be tuned into your customers' needs and focus your entire organization on fulfilling those needs.

How Are You Proving Your Commitment?

Ask yourself these questions:

- Have I set and articulated the specific baseline expectations of customer service for my organization?

- Do all of my customer communications (advertising, website, etc.) align with this expectation? Do we over-promise in any of our selling or marketing tools? Do both our new and current customers have a clear expectation of service?

- Do I have a clear set of guidelines defined for what to do when we fail to meet our customers' expectations? Does my team have the skills, training and autonomy to provide good recovery?

- Do my customers know what their options are when we fail? Have I trained my team to be as enlightened and well versed on these as I am?

- How are my compensation systems affecting the behaviors of my team toward customers? Am I rewarding the right behaviors?

- What information do we already have about our customers' impressions of our consistency and predictability when it comes to service? What can we do with that information to help us build better service for the future?

RULE 6

Invest In Your People

"Expect little and you will surely get it."
—Anonymous

Every minute of every day appalling customer service tales and tragic management stories are shared over coffee in cafés and distributed via blogs around the world. Yet a few of today's larger corporations—such as *Zappos*, *Virgin America* and *Edward Jones*—are leading the way to a brighter future with processes that keep their employees motivated and happy, and provide consistently remarkable service to a positively giddy (and growing) base of customers. Surely if these behemoths can pull together thousands of people to dazzle millions of customers we can do the same on a slightly smaller scale. I mean, all it takes is a strong leader, right?

Ahh, leadership. There was a time, not too long ago, when it felt as though great leaders in business, in our communities and on the world stage were plentiful. Today, many of us seem to be running our hands over our worry beads about the current lack of great leadership. But what exactly is it that we are longing for? What is it that differentiates a great leader from a mediocre one? And how can you, as a business owner, become the type of leader you need to be to woo customers and provide inspiration to your people? How can you create a style of leadership for your business that will attract the employees and customers you need to grow and profit?

In all my years working *for* and *with* entrepreneurs and business leaders across the country and around the world, I have come to the conclusion that truly effective leadership boils down to four seemingly simple directives: Engage, Inspire, Enable and Reward. These directives allow you to build an organization not populated by clones of yourself but rather one that grows with your vision and develops its own personality and processes for successfully wooing customers. If you consistently do these four things for your people you can and will succeed in weaving together a tightly knit organization that is capable of providing reliably superior service for a growing base of loyal customers.

Engage For Success

Whether you have been an entrepreneur for 20 days or 20 years, you know that it takes not only business acumen but also people acumen to create an engaged and customer-focused organization. You can have a dynamite product and well-honed processes but unless you engage your employees with the same level of passion you have for your company you won't be able to create a sustainable and scalable model for your business. If you want your company to grow proactively and profitably from your vision and your values you need to focus on creating the "village" that will get you there.

Hire For Attitude, Train For Tactics

If you run a company that deals directly with customers, hire people who like people. This point was driven home for me by six employees I interviewed in an effort to understand *Virgin America's* secret formula for customer service success. I set up the interviews because I wanted to know what was behind the incredibly positive experience I had with *Virgin America* flight after flight. How were they creating such a different experience from their competitors or frankly from 99 percent of the businesses I deal with as a customer every day?

All of the people I interviewed said that, while they weren't exactly sure why they were hired, they were sure their success in interviewing came from one thing ... their positive attitude. One of the flight attendants put it as simply as, "The difference seems to be in who *Virgin American* is hiring. I mean everything else is the same. We're trained the same way as we were at *Delta* and *United*, but the leadership here is invested in our having fun along with the passengers. It seems to be all about the people they choose to hire. I could never understand why everyone was so mean to customers. Being pleasant just seems natural to me. I really do enjoy coming to work and wanted to work for an airline that wanted me to have fun."

You can't teach attitude. Everyone knows that. Yet many of us spend valuable time considering prospective employees because they have a skill we won't have to spend time teaching them. And even though we intuitively know they don't have the right attitude or personality to be effective with our customers, we often hire them anyway. Whether or not you are hiring for a position that requires a specialized skill (one that simply can't be trained), your primary focus should be on finding someone with the kind of positive, caring and proactive attitude you yourself prefer to be greeted with when patronizing a business. Finding ways to actively filter for attitude at the front end of the hiring process doesn't have to be hard. You don't need a battery of expensive personality profiles—or even an interview. One resort client of mine found a brilliant solution when they were hiring from a large pool of candidates for a relatively small number of jobs.

Telluride Ski & Golf Resort
(www.tellurideskiresort.com)

Telluride Ski & Golf (TSG) prides itself on its guest service, its care of the environment, and its flare for fun. Each year, the company hires from a pool of generally younger workers many of whom haven't yet had the chance to learn what the phrase "customer service" means. Yet the people TSG hires are put in the most customer-centric position on the mountain, that of Lift Operator. From a pool of 1,300 applicants for only 250 jobs, Executive Director of Human Resources Heather Young and Executive Director of Guest Services Elizabeth Howe must find ways to weed out those who simply don't have a predisposition to providing a happy, engaged level of service. One recent year, rather than trying to judge personality from a one-page résumé or spend hour-upon-hour interviewing all 1,300 applicants, they decided to implement a very simple five-question survey that was to be completed along with each job application. The questions Young and Howe came up with were deceivingly simple yet elicited answers that told a great deal about the individual job applicants:

1. What have you done recently to impact the environment in a positive way?
2. If you had a free airline ticket to anywhere in the world, where would you go and why?
3. Who has been the biggest influence in your life and why?
4. What's the funniest thing that ever happened to you?
5. As an employee of TSG, how would you help improve our guest experience?

This seemingly simple survey was wildly successful for TSG because it accomplished a number of things. First, it ensured that only truly interested individuals applied because extra time and effort were required to complete the survey. Second, it shared with the applicants those aspects of the job that were most important for the organization. The seriousness with which the applicants approached their answers demonstrated the level of commitment those individuals might have to the organization. Third, the survey provided TSG with enough information to further delve into the important topics during a more formal interview. The result? Rather than wasting valuable managerial resources by interviewing 1,300 applicants, this simple questionnaire immediately eliminated over 850 applicants who wouldn't have been a good fit for the organization anyway!

Take a minute right now to consider how you might be able to refine your interview process. What questions are you asking your interviewees to get at how they feel about customers and serving them? Are you asking questions in the pre-interview stage that help you eliminate candidates who don't have the right attitude or outlook for the job? Is your hiring process truly focused on attitude and skills? Are you taking shortcuts so you don't have to spend time training or getting new hires "up to speed"? If so, how can you alter your process to produce better long-term results?

Create A Hiring Dialogue

Do you remember the last job you applied for? Did it end up being the job that was described to you or were you stunned to realize that 90 percent of what you were actually working on either wasn't described appropriately or, worse yet, wasn't even *in* the job description? Conversely, have you ever hired someone who, within a week of joining the organization, had already begun to show signs of not being a good fit for the position—either because of skill level or, as we discussed above, attitude? Personally, I believe the majority of hiring mistakes could be avoided if both the company and the prospective employee had a clearer picture of the position *before* the commitment was made. The next time you need to fill a position, take the time to reconsider what is actually required of the person who will play that role and create a dialogue with your interviewees about those items. Remember, a job description isn't an advertisement. You're not trying to *sell* the position; you're trying to *attract* the person who is most right for the job. Being frank and upfront about the job requirements will save you a lot of time and energy in the long run. Similarly, asking each applicant questions and considering the answers seriously will give you a chance to see how committed you are willing to be to this person. Hiring someone really is just like a marriage. The opportunities for success are greater if you actually know each other and haven't just met!

Test Drive Your Applicants

One of the most expensive, time consuming and important things you do as a business owner is hire people who will serve the internal and external customers of your organization. One of the most frustrating things you do is spend time and energy trying to "fix" hires that don't live up to your expectations. For this reason, allowing potential employees to try the position before either of you makes a commitment is a valuable investment of time and energy. Consider for a minute right now how you could put a process in place that would give potential hires the opportunity to work with you for a day or a week before a decision was made. Not only will their expectations for the job be set appropriately but also you will be able to see them in action and measure how much of a commitment you're willing to make to them.

Job Try-Outs

Ski resorts have a notoriously difficult time hiring people who are keenly focused on providing great service to their customers. Guests of ski areas interact with the Lift Operators more frequently than any other position on the mountain. Yet the job of operating the lifts is seasonal, low paying and requires you to stand outside in the cold weather for hours at a time without even an iPhone® to keep you company. The applicants for these positions tend to be younger people who are attracted to the job because of what they can do when they're *not* working (catch sick air in the fresh powder) rather than the experience they can offer the resort's customers. As a result, the ski industry has a whopping 30 percent failure rate in new hires for lift operations, not to mention astronomical costs for training, firing, and rehiring. But one of my resort clients tried a different approach to hiring Lift Operators that netted some surprising results.

After years of screening young people with little if any previous work experience the hiring manager was frustrated that so many applicants still, "didn't understand that when you get hired as a Lift Operator you actually have to *work* a *lift*." Apparently the Lift Operator title and job description weren't getting through. So she decided that, to find people who could not only withstand the trying physical conditions of this role but also achieve a level of service that would help the resort woo customers, they would need to approach hiring in a much different way. They had to find a way to make sure those applying really understood what they were getting themselves into. That year, the resort instituted a "test drive" program that allowed applicants who had made it through the initial screening and interviews to "spend a day on the slopes" and experience exactly what the job of Lift Operator entailed. This enabled the candidates to understand the rigors of the job more clearly. The hiring managers were able to more accurately gauge attitude as they watched the applicants interacting with customers and peers. And both those who were hired and their managers came to the partnership with more commitment as a result. In the end, the resort was able to increase their employee retention rate and reduce their firing and rehiring costs. Although the program lengthened the hiring process a bit the payoff later in the season made it all worthwhile.

Involve The Team In Hiring

One hiring fallacy I've never understood is that the person in charge of hiring for the company is the best person to judge that hire even if he or she is far removed from the work the individual will be required to do. I've even seen multi-million dollar companies that require the

CEO to approve all hires ... even those literally 10 levels below on the company's org chart. The truth is the best way to ensure the success of a new hire is to involve the team with whom he or she will be working in the hiring process. In other words, if you want your team to be invested in helping the new guy you need to allow them—no, *require* them—to be a part of finding and bringing that person on board. After all, who knows best what qualities and skills the position requires? Those who are doing the job already or working with that role every day!

The next time you have an opening, ask the team involved to get together and review the job description. Is it still relevant or has it changed as the company, customers, and market changed? Once the job description is posted, have your team review the résumés and interview the candidates *they* feel are most appropriate for the job. Once they have narrowed the field, give the remaining prospects the opportunity to test drive the role. After they have had a chance to try each other out, your team will have a great idea of who would be best for the role. If you feel the need, sure, go ahead and approve the hire through an interview yourself. But remember, it's the team's involvement that will cement your new hire's success. When they have an important role in choosing a new employee, your team members are less likely to allow that person to fail.

There Can Only Be One You

Quite a few entrepreneurs have sought my help because they were struggling to find a way to "duplicate"

themselves. Over and over again I've heard business owners lament their inability to find people who have the
same enthusiasm for exceptional service that they do. And
I get it. I really do. The irony is that, as an entrepreneur,
you have so much more control over whom you hire and
how you set them up to succeed than large multi-national
companies. So what's the secret? Put simply, it's a process
of filling in the blanks and looking for opportunities.
It's less about finding identical robots and more about
building a team of people with *complementary* skills and
attributes.

It's easy to make the mistake of hiring those who
think like you, sound like you, even look like you. But
diversity in background, in thought, and in perspective
is where the real value lies as you grow your organization. Don't get me wrong. You don't want to build a team
of rivals with completely different outlooks. But you do
want to find individuals who can help you see your people,
your processes, your products and even your marketplace
in fresh, new ways. If you've done your work early in the
hiring process you can set expectations—even before
you bring someone on board—about the contributions
they'll be asked to make as a member of the team. Tell
them exactly what behaviors you're looking for and what
role they can play in moving the business forward. The
more specific you are the better. "I'll need you to take
the initiative on a regular basis" doesn't help anyone.
But something like, "I'd like you to submit one new idea
each month for how we can increase safety on the job"
gives your new hire the opportunity to shine.

The key is to focus on what your prospective employee can bring to your mission of wooing customers. What unique attributes does he or she have that aren't already present on your team? Remember, true engagement begins not after you've hired someone but from the moment you envision the role you want that person to play. Alignment and involvement from creation of the job description to setting expectations enables your hires to begin wooing customers from day one.

Translate Vision Into Actions

Just like gears in a car, to move your business forward, your employees need to be fully engaged. They need to be deeply involved in winning, serving and cementing your relationships with customers. True engagement with your employees occurs when you are able to communicate your vision for the company and emotionally connect the individuals on your teams to that vision. It sounds easy but in reality, this is one of the most difficult things you will do as a leader. Getting to full engagement requires you to be specific about how your team can assist you in achieving the organization's goals. For example, one of your organization's goals might be to "increase customer loyalty." Well, that seems like a valid goal. But without specific information about what actions they need to take to achieve this, your team members may not be able to engage in the process. As their leader, you need to translate the vision of your organization into applicable, actionable and behavioral goals for the entire team. For example, an actionable goal that will likely lead to greater customer loyalty might be to "return customer calls within 24 hours." A specific goal like this is not only easy to execute but also easy for you to measure. Once your team is in line with how their behaviors directly link to the organization's goals, you will have true engagement.

Inspire Them To Be Their Best

Most of us think of inspiration as the "I Have A Dream" type of inspiration, the type of inspiration we feel when we see someone changing the world for the better or overcoming difficult odds to find success. But in reality, inspiration isn't reserved for the special few. Every one of us has the ability to inspire and be inspired. But it takes a catalyst to awaken those reserves and apply them to a greater goal. When it comes to your business, and wooing your customers, that catalyst is you. As a business leader, you need to find a way to inspire your employees and keep them in that mode because inspired employees create exceptional service and woo others to your cause. They serve both internal and external clients with zeal in an effort to do more, do it faster, do it with greater quality and do it to create something better. True inspiration allows your employees to rise to levels of performance even *they* didn't know they could attain.

Think of those moments in your life when you have felt the most inspired. My guess is that you saw yourself as a part of something bigger. To create this kind of inspiration in your workplace, you need to make sure everyone is clear about the vision and goals of the company *and* make sure everyone is playing a meaningful role in the greater effort to achieve your business goals. In other words, as a leader, you must provide the vision and also define the role each individual will play in the effort to bring that vision to life. Your people need to feel they are an important part of creating something bigger than themselves. Telling people they are important is not enough. Great leaders are those who allow others to help them attain their goals. This means you'll need to put your ego aside and give your team members the opportunity to be active participants in your success. It also requires ongoing maintenance—constant communication and discussion surrounding your organization's goals and your team's achievements, especially when times get tough. The first step in being a catalyst for this kind of inspiration is convincing the disbelievers that greatness is not only possible but also highly likely.

Instill A Belief In Greatness

Have you ever been working on something difficult or challenging and looked up suddenly to realize hours had passed rather than minutes? Have you ever looked back on an achievement and shaken your head wondering how you ever managed to accomplish it? Those are the moments during which a belief in the possibility of greatness has fueled your efforts and allowed you to achieve more than you thought you were capable of achieving. For several minutes, or several hours, you saw a clear vision of what you wanted to accomplish and you understood that you had what it would take to reach your goal. You were unstoppable. That kind of inspiration begins—for a team or an organization—when the individuals involved see the goal clearly *and* believe that the team has the ingredients it needs to achieve success.

A belief in greatness isn't accomplished through flowery rhetoric from a leader. Greatness does not simply materialize when you join a group with good cause. Trust me, there are plenty of private sector and public sector organizations that have legions of unhappy and disgruntled members even though they are working for a higher purpose or an enthusiastic leader. On the other hand, I have worked with literally hundreds of entrepreneurial organizations, both large and small, that have been able to inspire their members to go above and beyond for customers, for each other, and ultimately for the good of the organization—all because they believed they had what it would take to be great. What instills a belief in greatness is clarity of purpose *and* trust in the abilities of the individual members of the team. When your team members understand not only their own roles but also the roles of the other team members, you give them the ability to see the whole picture—to envision greatness happening—and that is what being an inspirational leader is all about.

Telluride Ski & Golf Resort

You've got a 1,000-person customer service force and one week to get them inspired. Ready? Go! That's what some businesses—such as ski resorts, golf resorts, summer camps—have to deal with at the start of every new season. *Telluride Ski & Golf Resort* had struggled for years with how to inspire their new seasonal employees—many who came from other towns—to do the basics of their jobs *and* provide the kind of service that would convince skiers and snowboarders to keep coming back year after year. Even though the company had state-of-the-art processes in place for tactical training they still weren't reaching the level of *inspiration* they needed to woo repeat customers. In the words of one leader, they just couldn't "... find a way to make sure these new employees had enough skin in the game."

Then, in 2008, *Telluride's* Jason Merritt, Employee Relations Manager and Heather Young, Executive Director of Human Resources decided to revamp their seasonal employee orientation program. Instead of the usual dry safety briefings and CEO speech, they shared the history of the town of Telluride from its early days as a booming mining town—through the mining bust—through the real estate boom and bust—and up to the beginning of the ski resort in 1973. They featured the numerous dedicated employees who were still with the resort 35 years after its inception and celebrated the resiliency of the town and its people. Then they painted a clear picture of how the loyalty of the customers and the success of the ski resort directly correlated with the survival of the town. They described with clarity the role each employee and each customer interaction played in making sure the town flourished. This orientation gave the new employees a clear understanding of the greater goals of the organization, defined the meaningful role each employee played and celebrated the belief that greatness for the town of Telluride was indeed possible if they all worked together. Throughout the season they kept the inspiration ball rolling by maintaining an ongoing dialogue about proactive steps employees could take to delight the ski resort's guests. As a result of their inspired efforts, the 2008–2009 ski season culminated in *Telluride Ski & Golf Resort* winning the prestigious National Ski Areas Association Customer Service Award.

Have A Passionate Purpose

I'm willing to bet your organization has a vision statement, a mission statement, a set of values and certainly business goals. But do you have a Passionate Purpose? You know, an emotional reason for doing what you do? Sure, you have a passion for your product or service—that's why you went into business—but what's behind that passion for you

> "Coming together is a beginning; keeping together is progress; working together is success."
>
> —Henry Ford

and your employees? In his book *Leadership And The Customer Revolution*, Gary Heil calls it a "Cause Worthy of Commitment."[11] Put yet another way, it's the thing that gets you out of bed each morning. Unlike financial or numeric goals, a Passionate Purpose is emotionally and inspirationally based.

The Passionate Purpose for your business isn't something you should come up with on your own. To ensure that it accurately reflects your whole business and that your employees buy in to it 100 percent, you should develop your Passionate Purpose together. If you have engaged the appropriate people and hired individuals who can contribute to your success, this shouldn't be rocket science. Simply set aside time to brainstorm and then work together to narrow down the options until you all agree on a statement that inspires and delights each one of you. It's a great team building exercise for your company and an important "success building" exercise for your business.

Work The Front Lines

As a business owner it's easy to get caught up in your leadership role and spend the better part of your time dealing with high maintenance customers or big-money clients. But if you ask me, you'd be far better off spending that time working the front lines. There are few things that create more inspiration for employees than seeing those in positions of power get in on the action. *Virgin America* insists its managers work the front lines with their employees every week. *Mt. Hood Meadows Ski Resort* asks all of its senior leaders to spend one morning a week doing the "everyday jobs that get the job done." You too should make a habit of rolling up your sleeves and going to work with your customers and front line employees at least once each week. Doing so will give you a better perspective on what it takes to perform each task in your organization. You'll be able to coach your employees more effectively because you understand, firsthand, what they're dealing with. You'll get a bird's eye view of your customers and how they interact with your employees and your systems so you can build more effective and efficient processes. You'll strengthen your team and their commitment to you. And you'll be in better touch with the wants and needs of your *Steady Eddies*, the bread and butter clients that fuel your success.

Talk About Your Customers

Yes, yes, the financials are important. But if that's all your employees hear you talking about, that's all they'll begin to care about. When employees see what is important to the boss, it's amazing how quickly that particular theme becomes a center of focus for them as well. And if you're not talking about your customers, why should they? As a business leader, you need to remember that the people who depend on you for their jobs are watching your every move and listening to every word you say—and *how* you say it. To ensure that your employees are getting the right signals with regard to wooing customers, you need to talk about your customers with your employees every single day. Not only that, but your discussions about customers must also be structured and productive. They must move you toward your business goals. When you talk to employees about customers in a productive way, you set an expectation for your employees to behave in a similar manner.

WRONG: *"Yeah, I know, she can be a real pain sometimes."*

RIGHT: "Boy, she always seems so stressed out. I wonder if there's something more we could be doing to help her."

WRONG: *"Hmph, he only spent a quarter what he usually spends with us. That's going to hurt our numbers."*

RIGHT: "Wow, he seems to be cutting back. Perhaps we should invite him in to talk about the recent changes in his business and how we might be able to assist him."

Great leaders don't just talk about customers in a way that sets the tone for their employees. They also work at helping their people look at things from the customer's perspective. Take a minute now to ask yourself if you're talking the talk *and* walking the walk. Are you speaking of customers with the respect and proactive attention to wooing that sets a good example for your employees? Are you engaging your people in an active conversation about what the world looks like from the customer's point of view?

Enable Great Things

Teams don't just come together and perform magically. As you've seen, it requires making a daily effort to inspire and engage your employees. But great leadership doesn't end there. To ensure your employees keep growing and reaching new levels of performance and achievement, you need to find ways to enable them.

Set Employee Expectations

The first step to positively enabling your team is—just as with customers—setting appropriate expectations. If your team members aren't clear about what you expect from them, you don't have a chance of getting them to a place where they can help you woo customers. By clear, I mean specific and actionable.

I was recently with a client who said his number one expectation for his employees was that they be "customer focused." After I heard that I went cube-to-cube and visited with 10 of his team members to ask them what "customer focused" meant. I got 10 totally different answers. None of the answers were necessarily wrong. But having a vague expectation that can be interpreted many different ways doesn't set a proper foundation for a company that needs to offer customers a consistent experience. It provides inconsistent and indistinguishable service, creating mere satisfaction at best and complete dissatisfaction at worst. Setting expectations for your employees requires you to define the individual players' roles (as we learned in Engage) and then apply measureable and achievable expectations to each role. Even individuals who are participating in the same activity may have different expectations based on their personal strengths. Remember, you want a well-rounded team, not a bunch of robots.

Teach Them The Dance Steps

Asking employees to create the kind of service experiences that woo customers without providing them with the necessary customer service skills to do so is like putting on music and asking someone to dance the tango when they have never been taught the steps. Certainly, many of us with enough observation and trial and error could probably dance a reasonable version of a tango. But wouldn't it be easier to do it well and become exceptional at it if we had someone there showing us the right steps and the right order? To truly woo your customers, you need to implement a formal program that helps your employees learn the basics of navigating your systems and procedures and more importantly, learn how and when to make good decisions around service. Without exception, world-class customer service teams are those who have been privy to not only the theory of customer service, but also the practical skills training that goes along with the theory. Again, doing training at your annual conference once a year isn't sufficient. You can bring trainers into your place of business; send employees to seminars and workshops; or even sign up for webinars that are held online and over the phone. You can develop your own half-day staff development programs or provide a couple of weeks of interactive instruction.

Set Your Poor Performers Free

While we're talking about enabling, we need to touch on the subject of poor performers. Everyone has a poor performer. And everyone thinks, "As long as I keep him or her away from customers it's not a big deal. Right?" Wrong! Nothing could be further from the truth. Not only do poor performers drive your customers away, they also affect the overall performance of the team. In a team of five, one poor performer can bring the overall productivity down by more than 40 percent![12] What's more, high performers tend to leave a team because they don't get enough time or training from their boss. If you are spending all your time with your poor performers, you have a 76 percent higher chance of losing your high performers. For the sake of your customers and your high performers, fire your poor performers now! In the long run it is fairer to the poor performer too because that person is more likely to pursue other avenues of employment and stumble upon something he or she is better at doing. If you have trouble taking action, consider creating an outplacement process that will help your poor performer transition to jobs where they can enjoy success.

Reward With Meaning

The moment I begin using the word "reward" most business leaders assume I mean monetary rewards. The statistics are overwhelming in this area and they aren't what you think. In most surveys conducted around the question, "How do you keep your most important employees happy and productive?" the results are clear. Money is usually *fourth* on a list of the five most important elements. Usually within that top four is a list of rewards that wouldn't cost your organization a penny. Believe it or not, they include things

> "Appreciate everything your associates do for the business. Nothing else can quite substitute for a few well-chosen, well-timed, sincere words of praise. They're absolutely free and worth a fortune."
>
> — *Sam Walton*

like: positive recognition, training, a clear idea of my career path, feeling cared about, flexibility in the work environment, additional responsibilities and challenges, being a part of decision making, and feeling of having a meaningful role. Yes, your employee compensation needs to be in the ballpark. But when it comes to enabling your employees to perform consistently well, a program that includes non-monetary rewards can be far more effective than adding a few dollars to their paychecks.

Just as you need to set individual expectations for your employees, you also need to consider reward types on an individual basis. Most of your employees will give clues as to how they would like to be rewarded. Suzy loves recognition in front of the group. Steve likes extra time off. And so on. Once you understand what motivates and excites your team members, it becomes easy to use those rewards to maintain and boost performance. I'm certainly not suggesting you have to reward every little triumph. The easiest way to create more of the behaviors you are looking for is to reward those behaviors. Think about how you like to be rewarded ... then, as a leader, observe and ask yourself, "How can I best reward each player on my team for a job well done?" It's that easy!

How Will You Keep The Commitment Alive?

Ask yourself these questions:

- What specifically am I doing during my hiring process to ensure I have the best chance of finding employees who fit my organization?

- Have I communicated my vision for the company to my whole team? Do they know my goals?

- Have I worked with my team to develop a Passionate Purpose that will help me achieve my goals?

- Am I taking the time to coach my employees and develop their customer wooing skills? Am I modeling the behaviors I want to see?

- What opportunities exist for me to "work the front lines" and how can I schedule that into my day in a way that allows me to interact with a full range of customers, not just the difficult ones?

- What's my plan to deal with my poor performers? Have I given them a fair chance to succeed by setting clear expectations, defining their roles on the team and providing measureable goals? If I have done all that and they are still not succeeding, what are my next steps in helping them find another place where they can be successful?

- What other opportunities exist for me to "reward" the wooing behaviors I see in my employees? What can I do "on the spot"? What can I do that will create long-term rewards?

RULE 7

✳ ✳ ✳

Run The Business;
Don't Let It Run You

"Think little goals and expect little achievements.
Think big goals and win big success."
— *David Joseph Schwartz*

"The achievement of your goal is assured the
moment you commit yourself to it."
— *Mack R. Douglas*

Getting used to the day-to-day responsibilities of being
an entrepreneur is no easy feat. Not only are you juggling your business, your financials, your customers, your
people but, oh yeah, you also have a life to live at some
point outside the walls of your business. So many small
businesses in America fail because people who are used
to the comforts of regular paychecks from big companies

get fed up with the politics and decide it would be "fun" to work for themselves. Don't get me wrong. Being an entrepreneur is awesome and thrilling and always interesting. But it's scary and heart wrenching too.

The greatest challenge an entrepreneur has is cutting through the noise to focus on the priorities that will move the business in the direction of opportunities for profitability and success. It sounds easy. But this can be a daunting task. When you have your own business, everything is a priority. It's easy to become overwhelmed by the sheer volume of "top priority" issues that come your way on a daily basis. How do you get your product created or your service bid out without losing track of your numbers, your people, your competitors? Chances are you started out—or are starting out—with a good idea that you believed you could make into a great company. But how do you take that same idea and woo your best and most profitable customers without letting the company run you?

Over the years I've met a great many leaders who all have their own individual styles but seem to use some similar guiding principles to maintain control of the business while living full and enriching lives. Here are a few things I learned from them.

Your Success, Your Terms

Every business owner has a different definition of success. Some want the freedom to work with whom they want and when they want, like Roberta Winchell in Rule 1. Some have a goal of creating a company that changes the way an entire industry works, like Reed Hastings from *Netflix*. Others simply have a great product or service they want to share. Those leaders who have been successful at creating businesses need to define what success looks like for them. Then create the structure that will allow them to do that.

My original goals were to create a business that would allow me to work with interesting, ethical and open business leaders who were looking for a way to improve performance. Over the years that goal has remained the same but I have added goals around the amount of time I need to be with my family, to travel, to write and to enjoy my personal life. Those added goals have helped me alter my business model to play more to my strengths. They've also required me to make some concessions with regard to income in order to gain that flexibility. Those are my terms of success. What are yours? Your terms may have some financial components, some customer components and some flexibility components. For the benefit of your employees and yourself, you need to be clear about what success looks like for you.

Be A Legendary Coach

One of the biggest mistakes you can make as a leader is wasting time managing tasks rather than leading and enabling your people. Clearly, you need to manage some administrative and company activities but your main emphasis must be on developing, coaching, training and enabling your team. This is the most important and usually the most overlooked element of an entrepreneur's work each day. It's so easy to get caught up in the latest crisis and run around in reactionary mode with your head on fire. But if you want to be successful and grow your business strategically, profitably and ideally to be less reliant on you, then you need to spend the same energy, passion and time helping your employees learn and grow every day. Great leaders spend over 80 percent of their time coaching, training and developing the individuals on their teams. Can you honestly say that's how you have been spending your time? If you don't feel you have enough time to coach/train/develop your people, then you need to take a hard look at where you *are* spending your time and consider adjusting your priorities. Perhaps you need to delegate or hire a manager to take over some of the day-to-day duties so you have time to focus on your people. Perhaps you aren't taking the time to step back from the day-to-day tasks long enough to come up with a strategy for shifting from a reactive leader to a proactive planner who is working to achieve long-term goals. When you spend all your time dealing with your organization's quotidian activities rather than focusing on developing your people, you are keeping your business and your employees from building your bottom line.

Coaching or "performance management" isn't as hard as the name implies. It simply requires taking a few moments each day to ensure you are talking with your team members about their skills and how they can be continuously improving them in order to achieve your organization's goals. Remember, performance management should never be a once-a-year review. That's simply not enough coaching time to build an employee's performance. Think about it. That would be similar to trying to learn to play golf or to ski with only one lesson. Don't you think you would learn faster if someone were watching and helping you build those skills every day? Great performance management conversations can take as few as two minutes and can have an enormous impact on your team's ability to succeed. These types of activities all help you enable your team members to learn, grow, be challenged *and* succeed.

As a coach for your employees you can offer them everything from an approving pat on the back to a specific one-on-one role-playing exercise. Every interaction you have with an employee is an opportunity for you to share your knowledge and skills in a way that will help that team member be better equipped to woo your customers. Great coaching conversations are specific and proactively help the recipients do something different to build their skills. A great coaching conversation is as easy as sharing three little pieces of information with your employee:

- Here's what you did really well ...
- Here's what didn't go as well as we would have liked ...
- Here's what you could do differently next time to get a better result ...

Trust Your Gut

If I had a dollar for every time my "gut" was right and I chose not to listen to it ... I would probably be retired on a beach somewhere enjoying a drink with an umbrella in it! Your gut instincts are the accumulation of all of your experiences, your perceptions and your realities from over the years. There's nothing magical about intuition. It really is simply your brain processing situations on multiple levels and at speeds that your conscious brain doesn't see. As an entrepreneur, your gut can be one of your most valuable tools ... but only if you listen to it. Brenda Rivers listened to her gut when she changed her business model for *Andavo Travel* even though everyone else in the industry "knew" it was a mistake. Jessie Boucher used her gut when she launched a business that served "lovingly prepared" home-delivered food into a marketplace where people seemed to be eating away from home with more and more frequency.

> "Intuition ... appears to be the extrasensory perception of reality."
>
> — *Dr. Alexis Carrel*
>
> "Common sense is instinct. Enough of it is genius."
>
> — *George Bernard Shaw*

I'm not suggesting you throw away your market analyses and business analytics. Those are important tools too. But I am suggesting that you take time to listen to that little voice in your head that tells you a certain path, a new product, a different market may be just the ticket. The trick to listening to your intuition is to be still. You need to give your unconscious mind time to assimilate the facts and provide you with that all-important "feeling" for the direction in which you should go. You need the time to absorb, analyze and sometimes discard data that you know "feels" wrong even though you can't explain why. To truly take advantage of all that your experience can provide, take the time

> "I feel there are two people inside of me—me and my intuition. If I go against her, she'll screw me every time, and if I follow her, we get along quite nicely."
>
> — Kim Basinger

to process and think. I'm not talking about going on a three-day silent retreat every time you need to make a business decision. But, when you feel that little twinge, that moment where you have discomfort about a decision, that's when you need to take a few minutes, take a deep breath and allow your gut to guide you. Trust me ... if you take the time to let your intuition have a say, you and your business will reap the rewards.

Your Time Is Your Money

When you work for someone else your priorities are often set for you, your projects assigned to you, and your time directed by others. When *you* are the boss your time (and the time of your team) really is *your* money. How you spend your time impacts not just your day but also your bottom line. Which means you can't afford to "wing it" through the day. You need to plan your activities carefully ... giving a great deal of thought to how the time you're spending is affecting your profitability.

One of my greatest struggles as my company has grown has been to let go of some of the day-to-day tasks that I not only enjoy doing but also like to have done "my way." Have you ever said (or maybe just thought), "Oh for Pete's sake! Just let me do it!" Even after 17 years running my business, even after teaching and writing about this topic every day, I can barely go a week without catching myself falling into those old controlling ways. But that's the trick ... catching yourself!

If you really want to shock yourself, do a little exercise right now. Take your To-Do list. Come on, I know you have one. Take that list and look at how many of the "tasks" are unrelated to building the profitability of your company for the long term. Now look at how few are related to wooing your customers. If you had to rethink your list right now and prioritize your activities using the following definitions, how would you be spending your time differently?

- *Wooing Activities*—Put a "W" next to any activity with a direct link to more effectively wooing your customers. Whether its documenting or improving a process so your team can better manage customer interactions or finding new marketing strategies that increase your ability to set the bar on customer expectations, or attending a conference on new and innovative ways to serve your customers ... if it's not building your profitability by creating better wooers and wooing it doesn't get the "W".

- *Only You Activities*—Put an "O" next to any activity that can only be done by you—either because you're the only one in your company or because the subject is confidential or proprietary. This might include performance evaluations, looking into a personnel matter or simply talking with an employee who's having a rough time. Remember, if an activity is only on your list because you haven't trained anyone or can't relinquish your need to do it yourself, it doesn't get an "O".

- *Other Activities*—Put a "Ø" next to any activity that doesn't fall into the above two categories. Find a way to get these items off your list and onto someone else's or eliminate the item altogether. Any time you spend on these items is time you don't get to spend working toward your goals. This includes all those "nice to do's" for your friends or old colleagues, baby showers (for anyone but your employees or customers), etc.

How's your list looking now? I ask you to follow this procedure for the next week. Be self-disciplined about attacking those "W" activities *first* and with gusto. Set time aside for them so you have the room to breathe and think. See if your business doesn't gain strength and profitability as a result. Your time is truly your money ... how are you spending yours?

Invest In Yourself

What about the activities that drive your productivity and build your strengths and your knowledge base?

Do they belong on the list? Indeed they do. But you have to begin to approach them in a different way than you may have in the past. Those list items that never seem to get done—like working out, going for a walk, calling an old client to catch up, attending that conference on a topic that you need to learn about for your business—are vital to your personal productivity. They are activities that only you can do, which means they belong in the second category, the "only you" category. But they deserve a different kind of attention than you have given them in the past. They deserve a higher level of importance. If you were a car that needed to drive across the country, wouldn't you want to make sure the tank was full, the tires were in good shape, the oil was changed and that you had the right maps in the glove compartment? A self-sacrificing entrepreneur is a self-defeating entrepreneur.

Rather than approaching personal care, wellbeing or individual growth activities as selfish luxuries you need to see them as a vital component of your profitability. Of course, not everything on your "To Do" list will get done. But *you* are the company asset over which you have the most control. The reality is that you won't take time to invest in yourself unless you schedule these activities with the same level of commitment as you would a customer call or an employee meeting.

If you know you have better focus and energy when you work out at the gym, then schedule it into your calendar and follow through on your appointment with yourself with the same focus that you follow through on a customer order. That's right, put it right on your calendar for all to see and have the discipline to make it happen. When you invest in yourself, you demonstrate your value to your employees and your customers.

As an entrepreneur I made it my policy to take time, at least once every six months, to attend a conference about my business or about one of my clients' businesses. I did this no matter how busy I was. And I never failed to return energized and full of ideas. These experiences allowed me to build my knowledge base by listening to and learning from the best and brightest people in their fields. My clients, in turn, were able to profit and gain from my increased knowledge. So remember, when you make the effort to think about your business in new ways, study the best practices of others and seek out people who inspire you and become cherished colleagues and friends, you're making an investment that's worth far more than that mundane task you considered doing instead.

Build Your Network

Everyone talks about building a network. Whole books have been written about how to create and manage a business network. You can even download an app from the Internet that allows you to "network" in real time with fellow passengers on your airplane! But what is the *real* return on investment for networking? And how do you make sure the networking you're doing is moving your business forward?

Remember, your time is your money. Which means you need to analyze your networking opportunities just as carefully as you would any other activity or time commitment. Every networking opportunity must be scrutinized for its ability to provide you and your business with increased profitability and opportunities for growth. As we learned in the previous section, entrepreneurs and small business owners have many more opportunities to attend conferences or belong to networking groups than just five or 10 years ago. But just as you can't be everything to everybody (in life or with your customers) you can't say yes to every networking opportunity either.

I certainly wouldn't go out and sign up for every group you can find. Rather, I would do some research on the array of options, events and activities available to you. Choose thoughtfully based on the activities that can provide you with the knowledge, skills, support and opportunities that will enable you to better woo current and future customers. Groups and organizations like the *Women Presidents' Organization (www.womenpresidentsorg.com)*, the *Young Presidents' Organization (www.ypo.org)*, *Make Mine a Million (www.makemineamillion.org)* or myriad others could help you connect, grow and thrive. When you consider the potential merits of networking with an individual or organization, make sure you are choosing those organizations, events, and people who will help you ...

- build your knowledge of your industry, best practices and/or customers;
- better find/connect to potential customers;
- create a confidential and supportive network to utilize for questions and issues in your business; and
- change the world.

If you're not sure who and what to choose, consider test-driving a selection of groups or events before you become a member. Or ask your friends, colleagues and clients about conferences and training opportunities they have attended. Put it on your list and do it today.

Remember The Joy

Remember that first big win your company ever had? Or the first day you opened your doors? That immediate and almost visceral jolt of joy you felt at being an entrepreneur? I believe remembering that moment, being able to relive it and conjure it up, even when times are tough, is what separates successful long-term entrepreneurs from those who become overwhelmed by the uncertainty and rollercoaster ups and downs every company faces over its lifetime. Great entrepreneurs not only have to maintain their enthusiasm for the work and their people but also for their customers.

Entrepreneurs who can successfully woo customers for the long term bring a little bit of joy to the job every day and with every interaction—with employees, prospects, customers and even their friends. Let me be clear here. I'm not referring to the "cheerleading" kind of joy that almost always feels insincere and can be excruciating to be around. I mean the type of joy that allows people to do their best because they feel their best. This is the type of joy that comes from seeing a great product transform the lives of happy customers. The type of joy that manifests itself when you know you're doing something you're passionate about and you get a little bit better at doing it every day ... for your customers, for your employees and yourself.

When times are tough, when you have to make difficult decisions or tough strategic choices, find a way to take a moment to reflect on why you first went into business. What was it that you wanted to build, grow, or contribute? What "got you into this mess" to begin with? As you reflect back to those moments of triumph and possibility, consider what got you there. What actions did you take? What strengths did you build upon? What tactics did you employ that allowed you to achieve that success? Is there a way to use those tactics in this situation? Remember, your greatest assets are the strengths you bring to the table. Get conscious of how those play into your successes, large and small, every day and you will become a master at wooing your customers and wooing success.

What's Your Happy Ending?

Ask yourself these questions:

- What does success look like for me? How would I define success on *my* terms? Am I clear about what this journey looks like?

- What commitment can I make to myself that will allow me the time to listen to my "gut?" What time can I set aside each week to ensure I have the space to hear my intuitive voice?

- What's on my "To Do" list? Are they *Wooing* activities? *Only Me* activities? What items can I eliminate or delegate to someone else? How can I make that change today?

- How am I investing in my own wellbeing? How am I expanding my knowledge base? What am I doing weekly? Bimonthly? Annually?

- What organizations and groups could I enlist to help build an intelligent network? Am I participating in ineffective or unfair networking? What is my plan to remedy that?

- What's the most "joyful" business memory I have? What did I do to make that come about? What can I learn from that success that can help me today? Tomorrow?

End Notes

1. Reichheld, Frederick F., and Thomas Teal. *The Loyalty Effect: The Hidden Force Behind Growth, Profits, and Lasting Value.* New Ed ed. New York: Harvard Business School Press, 2001. Print.

2. "Toyota Slips Up." *The Economist* 12 Dec. 2009: 11. Print.

3. "Losing its shine." *The Economist* 12 Dec. 2009: 75–77. Print.

4. Ayres, Chris. "Revenge Is Best Served Cold—On YouTube: How a broken guitar became a smash hit." *Times Newspapers Ltd.* [London] 22 July 2009: *www.timesonline.co.uk*. Web. 9 Mar. 2010.

5. Carlzon, Jan. *Moments of Truth—New Strategies for Today's Customer-Driven Economy.* Boston: Ballinger Publishing Company, 1987. Print.

6. San Francisco Business Times. *The Top Reason Customers Leave.* American City Business Journals, Inc. October 17, 1997.

7. Weingarten, Mark. "Designed to Grow." *Business 2.0* June 2007: 35–37. Print.

8. Chafkin, Max. "Get Happy." *Inc.* May 2009: 67–73. Print.

9. "A Social Networker's Story: The Zappos CEO and UPS Step In." *Businessweek* 2 Mar. 2009: 30. Print.

10. Magnini, VP et. al., *"The service recovery paradox: justifiable theory or smoldering myth?"* Journal of Services Marketing 21, no. 3 (2007): 213–225. Print.

11. Heil, Gary, Tom Parker, and Rick Tate. *Leadership and the Customer Revolution: The Messy, Unpredictable, and Inescapably Human Challenge of Making the Rhetoric of Change a Reality.* New York: Wiley, 1995. Print.

12. Schmidt, Frank L., and John Hunter. *Individual Differences in Productivity.* New York: Journal of Applied Psychology, Volume 68, no. 3 (1983). Print.

Index

Acknowledgments

This book would never have been written without the selfless, passionate and brilliant assistance of my editor and co-conspirator Nancy Holland Hellmrich. My gratitude also goes to Beth Edwards and Emma Pizzardi for their faith in me and their support during this process. So many others offered their extraordinarily generous help with various aspects of this project including Michel Hogan, Jennifer McLellan, Jennifer Nicholas and Cynthia Martin. I also have to thank the amazing entrepreneurs who shared their stories of success with me, including Jessie Boucher, Heather Young, Roberta Winchell, Angie Hofelich and Matthew Drake. I would also like to thank the most extraordinary entrepreneur and friend whose support and love over the years has helped make me a better entrepreneur and person—Brenda Rivers.

My sincerest appreciation goes to the women of KeyBank including Maria Coyne, Elizabeth Henton and the amazing Melissa Smolko who helped inspire me to write this book. Were it not for KeyBank and their magnificent Key4Women program this book would simply not have been possible. Key4Women is a nationwide network of entrepreneurial women who share a passion for business and a perspective on success. The program is dedicated to helping women take advantage of every business opportunity that can be discovered and to creating new ones along the way. Finally, special thanks to all of my past and present clients for the experiences and insights that provided the wisdom and intelligence that became *The Rules of Woo.*

About The Author

Cindy Solomon

Internationally Recognized Speaker,
Consultant, Facilitator & Author

Cindy Solomon is one of the most sought after leadership and customer loyalty speakers in the country. Over the past 15 years, she has helped thousands of individuals and hundreds of organizations build bottom line results by creating profitable, long-term relationships with their customers and employees. Working with clients as diverse as *Cisco, Genentech, State Farm Insurance* and *Microsoft,* Cindy brings her irreverent and results oriented take on creating customer and employee loyalty to thousands of leaders every year.

As President of *Solomon & Associates, Inc.,* Cindy works with hundreds of companies a year to help them align all aspects of their organization toward the goal of wooing lifelong customers and developing highly effective employees thus building truly customer-focused organizational cultures. She is known for her witty, motivational and fully customized delivery, which allows business leaders to build their knowledge base, while building their enthusiasm for productive change, lifelong learning and exceptional customer service.

Solomon's insights have appeared in *PINK* magazine, *More* magazine, *The Denver Business Journal, NSAA* magazine, *NGCOA* magazine, *The Naked Truth: A Manifesto for Working Women, The Transparency Edge, Women On Top*, and more. For more about Cindy Solomon and *Solomon & Associates, Inc.*, visit *www.cindysolomon.com*.